ALMOST ALCOHOLIC

JUL 17 2012

ALMOST ALCOHOLIC

Is My (or My Loved One's) Drinking a Problem?

Robert Doyle, MD, Harvard Medical School

Joseph Nowinski, PhD

HAZELDEN®

Hazelden
Center City, Minnesota 55012
hazelden.org

© 2012 by Harvard University
All rights reserved. Published 2012
Printed in the United States of America

No part of this publication may be reproduced, stored in a retrieval system, or transmitted in any form or by any means—electronic, mechanical, photocopying, recording, scanning, or otherwise—without the express written permission of the publisher. Failure to comply with these terms may expose you to legal action and damages for copyright infringement.

Library of Congress Cataloging-in-Publication Data

Doyle, Robert (Robert L.)
Almost alcoholic : is my (or my loved one's) drinking a problem? / Robert Doyle, Joseph Nowinski.
p. cm.
Includes bibliographical references.
ISBN 978-1-61649-159-8
1. Alcoholism. 2. Alcoholism—Prevention. I. Nowinski, Joseph. II. Title.
HV5060.D69 2012
362.292—dc23
2011048213

Editor's note

The names, details, and circumstances have been changed to protect the privacy of those mentioned in this publication.

This publication is not intended as a substitute for the advice of health care professionals.

Alcoholics Anonymous, AA, and the Big Book are registered trademarks of Alcoholics Anonymous World Services, Inc.

16 15 14 13 12 1 2 3 4 5 6

Cover design by Teresa Jaeger Gedig
Interior design and typesetting by Kinne Design

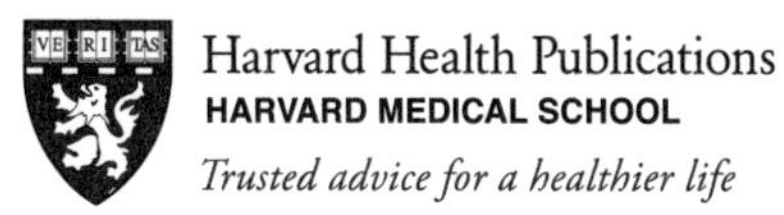

***The Almost Effect*™ series** presents books written by Harvard Medical School faculty and other experts who offer guidance on common behavioral and physical problems falling in the spectrum between normal health and a full-blown medical condition. These are the first publications to help general readers recognize and address these problems.

For Angelina, Frances, Sandra, Ellen,
and Elizabeth from R. D.

and

for Maggie, Becca, and Greg from J. N.

contents

series foreword

The Almost Effect

I once overheard a mother counseling her grown daughter to avoid dating a man she thought had a drinking problem. The daughter said, "Mom, he's not an alcoholic!" The mother quickly responded, "Well, maybe not, but he *almost* is."

Perhaps you've heard someone, referring to a boss or public figure, say, "I don't like that guy. He's *almost* a psychopath!"

Over the years, I've heard many variations on this theme. The medical literature currently recognizes many problems or syndromes that don't quite meet the standard definition of a medical condition. Although the medical literature has many examples of these syndromes, they are often not well known (except by doctors specializing in that particular area of medicine) or well described (except in highly technical medical research articles). They are what medical professionals often refer to as subclinical and, using the common parlance from the examples above, what we're calling *the almost effect.*

For example:

- Glucose intolerance may or may not always lead to the medical condition of diabetes, but it nonetheless increases your risk of getting diabetes—which then increases your risk of heart attacks, strokes, and many other illnesses.
- Sunburns, especially severe ones, may not always lead to skin cancer, but they always increase your risk of skin cancer, cause immediate pain, and may cause permanent cosmetic issues.
- Pre-hypertension may not always lead to hypertension (high blood pressure), but it increases your risk of getting hypertension, which then increases your risk of heart attacks, strokes, and other illnesses.
- Osteopenia signifies a minor loss of bone that may not always lead to the more significant bone loss called osteoporosis, but it still increases your risk of getting osteoporosis, which then increases your risk of having a pathologic fracture.

Diseases can develop slowly, producing milder symptoms for years before they become full-blown. If you recognize them early, before they become fully developed, and take relatively simple actions, you have a good chance of preventing them from turning into the full-blown disorder. In many instances there are steps you can try at home on your own; this is especially true with the mental and behavioral health disorders.

So, what exactly is the almost effect and why this book? *Almost Alcoholic* is one of a series of books by faculty members from Harvard Medical School and other experts. These books are the first to describe in everyday language how to recognize and what to do about some of the most common behavioral and emotional problems that fall within the continuum between normal and full-blown pathology. Since this concept is new and still evolving, we're proposing a new term, *the almost effect*, to describe problems characterized by the following criteria.

The problem

1. falls outside of normal behavior but falls short of meeting the criteria for a particular diagnosis (such as alcoholism, major depression, antisocial personality disorder, or substance dependence);
2. is currently causing identifiable issues for individuals and/or others in their lives;
3. may progress to the full-blown condition, meeting accepted diagnostic criteria, but even if it doesn't, still can cause significant suffering;
4. should respond to appropriate interventions when accurately identified.

The Almost Effect

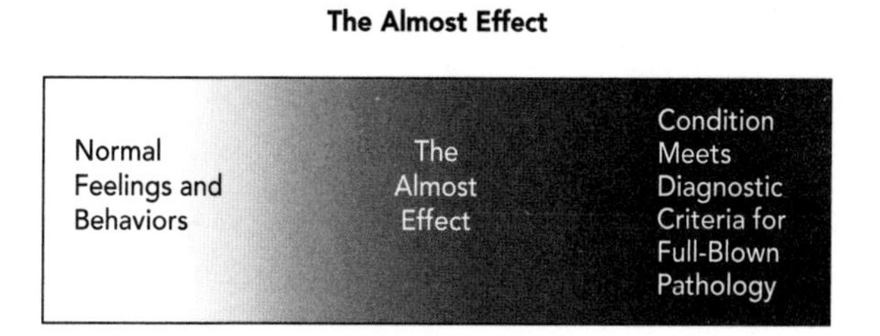

All of the books in The Almost Effect™ series make a simple point: Each of these conditions occurs along a spectrum, with normal health and behavior at one end and the full-blown disorder at the other. Between these two extremes is where the almost effect lies. It is the point at which a person is experiencing real pain and suffering from a condition for which there are solutions—*if* the problem is recognized.

Recognizing the almost effect not only helps a person address real issues now; it also opens the door for change well in advance of the point at which the problem becomes severe. In short, recognizing the almost effect has two primary goals: (1) to alleviate pain and suffering now and (2) to prevent more serious problems later.

I am convinced these problems are causing tremendous suffering, and it is my hope that the science-based information in these books can help alleviate this suffering. Readers can find help in the practical self-assessments and advice offered here, and the current research and clinical expertise presented in the series can open opportunities for health care professionals to intervene more effectively.

I hope you find this book helpful. For more information about other books in this series, visit www.TheAlmostEffect.com.

Julie Silver, MD
Assistant Professor, Harvard Medical School
Chief Editor of Books, Harvard Health Publications

acknowledgments

The authors wish to express their appreciation to Julie Silver, MD, of Harvard Medical School and Harvard Health Publications, and to Sid Farrar of Hazelden Publications for their invaluable editorial assistance at every step of the process of producing this book, from its initial conceptualization to the final product. We also want to thank Iva Pravdova, MD, and Carol Dyson, RN, for sharing their insights on the generational effects of alcohol and substance abuse in families. Finally, we'd like to thank our literary agent, Linda Konner, for her support of and commitment to this book and The Almost Effect series.

introduction

Normal and Abnormal Drinking

We are two doctors—a psychiatrist and a psychologist—who have worked as mental health professionals for many years. In addition, each of us has pursued further training in the area of substance abuse. We were privileged to have learned from experts in some of the best treatment centers in the world, including the Betty Ford Center and the Hazelden Foundation.

By way of introduction, Dr. Rob Doyle is a psychiatrist who works for Harvard University Health Services. Besides providing mental health medical care to Harvard students, he is involved in research and is a frequent speaker at workshops and conferences. Dr. Joe Nowinski, a clinical psychologist, works for the University of Connecticut Health Center. He also is involved in research in substance abuse treatment and has trained many clinicians in the interventions he has developed.

In this book, we will share an important revelation that we have learned from our collective experience. This revelation has not been described in other books or even in the medical literature. Nevertheless, it has enormous impact on the lives of millions of people. Here's what we've discovered: the men and women who have been diagnosed as alcohol dependent—or, more simply, alcoholic—represent but the tip of the iceberg of a much larger segment of the population whose lives are negatively impacted by alcohol use. One way to think of those who carry an official alcohol-related diagnosis is that they fit fairly neatly into a diagnostic "box" defined by various objective symptoms. But what about this other group—the much larger part of the iceberg that lies below the waterline? Though not technically alcoholics, these men and women—young, middle-aged, and older adults—nevertheless are experiencing problems related to their drinking. There is pain and suffering going on that is undiagnosed—and untreated—simply because it hasn't really been described or defined.

We call these people "almost alcoholics" and this is the first book that identifies and explains this condition. The "almost" concept is a paradigm shift in the way we look at alcohol use. Put simply, the "almost alcoholic" does not drink normally but also wouldn't be labeled an "alcoholic." Because this is a new concept to many people, they often don't see the connection between their drinking and the various problems it is causing. Similarly, the doctors or other professionals they consult with may not connect the dots either. The result is that quite a few of these men and women will continue to suffer the consequences of their drinking—consequences that not only affect them directly, but have a powerful ripple effect and cause considerable suffering to those around them as well. Such consequences may include failed romantic relationships, alienation of children and parents, careers marked by underachievement, declining health, and emotional problems. Eventually, for some of these people, their drinking will progress to the point where they will be diagnosed as alcoholics and will hopefully get help. But even if they don't reach this point, the significant, unaddressed suffering of the person who is almost alcoholic can be relieved by recognizing the problem and then addressing it.

In this book, we help you understand what it means to be an almost alcoholic—whether that term applies to you or to someone you care about—and we give you some practical, proven suggestions on what you (or your loved one) can do about it. If you are concerned about another person, we encourage you to share this book with him or her. You might suggest keeping a journal to answer the questions that appear in the book; they are designed to help people assess and make good decisions about their drinking.

Either way, let's start by taking a look at cultural values around alcohol use, and with that as background, we can begin to explore the difference between almost alcoholics and true alcoholics.

Social Drinking, Almost Alcoholics, and Alcoholics

Drinking alcoholic beverages—at least in a social context—has been part of many cultures for centuries. The United States is no exception. You need only turn on a Sunday afternoon football or baseball game on television to witness a seemingly endless array of commercials showing men and women having a great time together, snacking and downing cold beers. Those images convey that drinking is a normal, fun social activity. Indeed, for many people pizza and beer, cocktails, or wine and cheese—enjoyed in the company of friends, at the ballpark, at a happy hour, or in a sports bar—are a routine part of a normal social life.

Okay, if you're not an alcoholic and social drinking is a normal part of life—what's the problem? Why write this book? Very simply, because we've learned that a certain percentage of those men and women who are enjoying themselves watching games and drinking cold beers (or enjoying wine and cheese with friends) will at some point cross a line—a line they will most likely not recognize—and become what we're calling almost alcoholics. The reason they will not realize what they have done is that the line separating normal social drinking from being almost alcoholic is not bright and sharp, but is more of a gray area that people can venture into before they know what's happened.

We know that some people who start drinking will never be "normal" or social drinkers and will go on to become true alcoholics. What does that mean? Essentially, it means two things. First, the true alcoholic will inevitably reach a point where one drink is never enough. Once true alcoholics reach this stage, when they start drinking, they rarely stop until they're drunk. Second, alcoholics do not feel normal without some amount of alcohol circulating in their bloodstream. As soon as their blood alcohol level gets low, they start craving a drink. And since one drink is never enough, stopping once they've started drinking is not an option. These constitute two of the core "symptoms" that have classically defined alcoholism. They are key elements in the diagnostic "box" that most professionals (and insurance companies) use to decide who needs treatment for alcohol dependence.

Of course, alcoholism is not diagnosed simply by these two concepts. There is a longer list of criteria, put forth by the American Psychiatric Association and the American Medical Association. In the next chapter, we list these criteria and compare them to our criteria for almost alcoholism. Alcohol dependence represents one extreme on a spectrum that ranges from normal social drinking to true alcoholism. Alcoholism is a much more severe problem and is associated with much more severe consequences than *almost* alcoholism, which occupies a large "zone" between normal social drinking and alcoholism.

As two mental health professionals specializing in treating people with alcohol and drug problems, we have diagnosed and worked with many true alcoholics. We know they have a disease and need help. Many of them recover and go on to lead very productive lives. But this book is about almost alcoholics and, although this condition has not been well studied, we estimate that for every alcoholic who fits the official diagnostic criteria for alcoholism, there are many others who "almost" fit the criteria and are, therefore, *almost* alcoholics. Their problems are usually not as severe as the problems faced by alcoholics, but they are nonetheless real and can have devastating effects on the lives of almost alcoholics and the people around them.

Our clinical experience is supported by research conducted by the National Institute on Alcohol Abuse and Alcoholism. According to the NIAAA, the percentage of Americans who may not be alcoholics but whose self-reported drinking is enough to qualify them as having problems that can be linked to drinking has been on the increase for at least a decade.[1] It is among this group of people that we find the *almost alcoholics*.

Drinking Is Seldom the Reason People Seek Help

When almost alcoholics come to one of our offices, it is usually *not* for help with what they see as a drinking problem. Rather, they may be having trouble managing a teenage child. Or they may complain that their marriage seems in danger from too much fighting and too little sex. Sometimes they come to us because they've been feeling depressed or anxious for a long time or have been suffering from chronic insomnia. Many of them have said that a few drinks at the end of the day helped them to relax or fall asleep, only to find in time that the drinks no longer produced this effect.

You will meet some of these people in this book. The case examples are drawn from our own professional experience, but we have changed names and other identifying features to protect the privacy of those involved. Some characters are composites.

Some almost alcoholics seek help for a medical issue, again without seeing the connection between drinking and their symptoms. Matt was one of these people. A forty-five-year-old sales executive, Matt considered himself successful—at least in his work. Divorced and with an eight-year-old daughter, Matt spent a lot of time on the road, so much so that he said, "I think of airports as my office." He was as connected as anyone we'd heard of and was capable of hosting online meetings while waiting for his flight to board.

Matt made an appointment with his doctor when he noticed, to his considerable distress, that his hands and feet "tingled" and sometimes became numb. His doctor sent him to see several specialists, including a hematologist, a rheumatologist, and a neurologist. Initially, the tests all came out clear, but then he had nerve and muscle studies (sometimes referred to as

EMGs or electromyograms) to test for nerve damage. These tests revealed injury to the nerves in his hands and feet, called a *peripheral neuropathy*. There are many things that can cause a peripheral neuropathy, including alcohol. In most cases, so-called alcoholic neuropathy takes a long time to become evident, which is why a doctor might not suspect it in a man of forty-five. However, some cases of alcohol-related neuropathy have been associated with acute and rapidly progressive onset.

After getting these test results, Matt's doctor met with him for nearly an hour and did an in-depth assessment. It was during that assessment that Matt disclosed that he'd been in the habit of drinking three or four beers a day—plus an occasional cocktail or two—every day except those days when his daughter visited with him, which given his extensive business travels amounted to no more than five or six days a month. Moreover, he'd been drinking that much for many years. But he never missed a day of work, never had a blackout, and was able to "hold his liquor" well so that people around him never realized he was in fact intoxicated.

Being just forty-five, it had never occurred to Matt that he could be suffering from serious medical problems due to his drinking, and the possibility only emerged when his doctor conducted a thorough inquiry. When his doctor referred Matt back to the neurologist with this added information, further tests revealed that Matt was indeed suffering from a peripheral neuropathy that was most likely caused by his drinking. Matt's doctor also told him there was a chance that his neuropathy could be arrested, and perhaps even reversed, but only if Matt abstained from drinking. Given the dire situation he found himself in, Matt decided to do just that. A year later, he was able to report to his doctor that, while he still had occasional bouts of numbness or tingling in his hands and feet, they had indeed become less frequent and severe since he'd stopped drinking.

Social Drinking and Almost Alcoholic Drinking

Matt's story and many others like his have brought this large group of previously undiagnosed individuals to our attention. As diverse as their stated reasons for seeking help may be, the common denominator for many of these people could be described as "social drinking gone over the line." In other words, they've crossed into that gray area that separates normal drinking from alcoholic drinking.

Although there's a strong correlation between their alcohol use and the problems we have described, our experience is that most almost alcoholics see no connection between the problems and their drinking. They are unable to "connect the dots." We're not really surprised, for two reasons. First, because little has been written about crossing the line separating normal social drinking from almost alcoholic drinking, it represents a new and novel concept to most people.

The second reason is that this change—moving from normal social drinking to almost alcoholism—doesn't happen suddenly. Rather, it typically is a slow and insidious change, one that is so subtle and gradual as to be virtually undetectable to those who are experiencing it (as well as to those who are close to them). From what we have seen, this process can take years and can be so gradual that those affected never see a reason to consult with a doctor or counselor, much less change their drinking behavior. Yet others around them—spouses, other family members, friends, colleagues, employers—often do see the problems caused by the drinking, even if they don't recognize the drinking as a contributing factor. Sometimes it is pressure from these people that drives the almost alcoholic (reluctantly) to give us a call.

• • •

What are we asking of you, the reader? Basically, we are asking you to keep an open mind as you read this book. We are not saying that social drinking will always lead to problem drinking, and we are not trying to put labels on people where there isn't a problem. Instead, our goal is to recognize, acknowledge, and support people who are experiencing—and causing—real suffering with their almost alcoholic drinking. What we are saying is that we know there is a gray zone beyond social drinking, and this gray zone is the place where some social drinkers become almost alcoholics. We want to help you decide whether that has happened to you or to someone you love. If it has, we have some strategies that may help.

Part 1

Understanding the Almost Alcoholic

1

What Is *Almost Alcoholic*?

Geraldo, thirty-eight, had worked in the commercial real estate development field since graduating college with a degree in business management. His employer had offices and developed properties in the New England area. For many years the firm did nothing but grow, and Geraldo advanced along with it. He was now in charge of overseeing the budgets for new projects in three states. There was only one problem: for the last three years the number of new projects that the company was able to win contracts for had steadily dwindled as the US economy sank into a protracted slump.

Part of Geraldo's job involved traveling to the various project sites. There, he'd get a sense for whether the project was on schedule, which in most cases also meant that it would be on budget. His employer had found that being on site was the best way to monitor this activity. It was a strategy that had proven successful over time.

When Geraldo traveled, he lived on an expense account.

The company put him up in moderately priced hotels and paid a reasonable daily stipend for food. Geraldo also could do some entertaining of customers, mostly taking them to dinner or out for drinks. It was in this context that Geraldo found himself becoming an almost alcoholic.

Geraldo's drinking was not excessive—at least not in his own mind. And if you were to ask the customers he entertained, it's doubtful that any of them would say he ever got drunk. Nevertheless, Geraldo, who ten years earlier was someone who would only drink a cocktail or two on weekends, was now a man who had one or two cocktails almost every night—whether he was traveling or not. Was this a problem? Not from Geraldo's point of view. He'd never, for example, even considered that he might be a "problem drinker." On the other hand, Geraldo's habit of fixing himself a cocktail (and then a second) as soon as he got home from the office meant that he usually preferred to watch the news on television instead of helping with or overseeing his two preteen daughters' homework. Between his business travel and his "cocktail hour," Geraldo's interaction with his daughters had dwindled steadily. His wife had started to notice and had remarked on it more than once.

The bad economy was also creating added stress on Geraldo at work. In order to keep making a profit and avoid possible layoffs, the firm needed to be sure it could reap maximum profits from each of its remaining projects. This meant the pressure was on Geraldo, and one way he responded was to drink one or two glasses of wine at lunch when he was traveling, in addition to his regular cocktails. Again, did that make Geraldo an alcoholic? No. On the other hand, and while he did not really notice it, Geraldo was not as cognitively sharp and on the ball after lunch as he was before lunch. And that had led to a couple of projects falling behind both in terms of schedule and cost. Geraldo knew these slips could mean trouble for him if they weren't corrected. That worry was starting to keep him up at night.

We would describe Geraldo as an *almost alcoholic*, and he definitely could use some help. Let's look at why.

Two Kinds of People, or Many Different Shades?

Some people believe there are only two kinds of people in the world: alcoholics and nonalcoholics. The generally accepted criteria for diagnosing people with alcohol use issues has supported this concept. Moreover, many people also believe that we are either born alcoholics or we are not. This has been a prevailing view for a long time, and although this statement may seem dramatic to some, it does have some basis in reality. That basis is the fact that those who hold these beliefs tend to be people who have experienced or witnessed the most severe symptoms and/or the most severe consequences of drinking. These symptoms and consequences include the following:

- Being unable to stop drinking, beginning from the first time he or she had a drink
- Repeatedly having blackouts (i.e., not remembering the next day what happened) after having only a few drinks
- Being arrested multiple times for driving while intoxicated
- Becoming violent on more than one occasion when drinking

We know from our own clinical experience that there are people who develop severe alcohol drinking patterns and behaviors such as the ones just described. Of those people who are admitted into inpatient alcohol treatment programs, a large majority have experienced problems such as those just described. They are true alcoholics. Fellowships such as Alcoholics Anonymous were founded by and for these very people—the so-called hopeless cases. It isn't hard to understand, then, why some people (including many health care professionals) conclude that there are only two kinds of people in the world: alcoholics and nonalcoholics. If we were to draw a picture of such a vision of "the drinking world" it would look like this:

The Drinking World

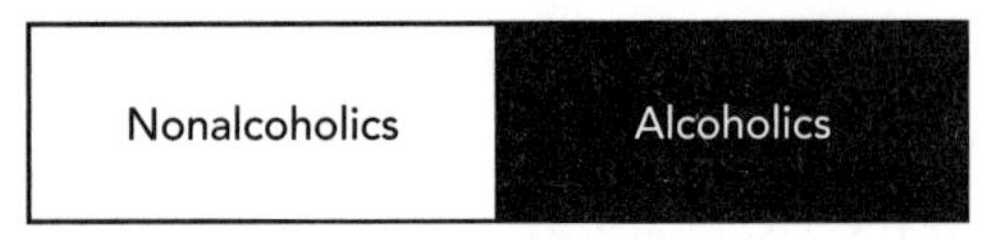

Anyone who drinks heavily is at risk for adverse health consequences, but some people appear to face a heightened risk for developing alcohol-related health problems. The reason appears to be largely biological, although environmental factors also likely play a role in this difference. In support of this biological argument, researchers have found, for example, that people differ in how their bodies metabolize alcohol. Since our biological makeup is determined at birth, there is some truth in the idea that we have certain traits that make us more (or less) vulnerable to the effects of alcohol.

Our discovery of the almost alcoholic came through our many years of working not only with people who had the kinds of drinking problems just described, but also with a much larger group of people with a variety of drinking patterns that didn't meet the criteria for alcoholism. As noted earlier, the majority of this larger group came to us not because they were concerned (or because others had expressed concern) about their drinking, but for help with some other problems. The connection between the problems they sought help for and their drinking emerged only later. Let's look at a couple more examples.

Jennifer's Story

Jennifer, age forty-one, was married with two children, an eleven-year-old son and a nine-year-old daughter. Jennifer's was a typical, two-income contemporary family. She had a middle-management job in a large real estate development and management company, while her husband, Dan, worked in the information technology department of a large university. As was true for most of the couples they knew, they struggled with balancing the demands of work with those of parenting, not to mention housekeeping. They enjoyed their life in a comfortable suburban community with good schools and access to recreation; at the same time, both Jennifer and Dan sometimes expressed that they found life on a "treadmill" difficult.

Dan and Jen had met in college during their junior year and married a year after graduating. As college students, they'd enjoyed partying as much as most of their friends, but had never gone "over the top" with it. They'd each known the occasional hangover, especially as freshmen, and both enjoyed meeting friends for tailgating parties at football games after graduation.

Jen did not drink at all during her pregnancies. However, after her second child was born, and after she returned to work following a six-week maternity leave, she joined Dan in his routine of sipping a glass of wine while they "decompressed" after work. That meant unloading the kids, making dinner, supervising homework, getting ready for the next day, and so on. Then after the kids were in bed, Jen would have a second glass of wine, and sometimes a third. She told us that for a number of years this was an effective way for her to release the stress that built up over the course of the day. She also felt that the third glass of wine helped her sleep better.

When Jen sought therapy, it was not because of her drinking—which she still regarded as normal, and indeed helpful, given her high-pressure lifestyle. Jen was referred by her primary care physician, with whom she had shared her concerns about not sleeping well. Not sleeping well left her feeling "wired" the next day. That pattern then led her to feel increasingly depressed, which was reflected in a shortened temper (especially with the children), chronic feelings of fatigue, and a complaint from Dan that their sex life was "evaporating." She'd asked her doctor about sleeping medications, or perhaps an antidepressant. The doctor said she would consider that, but first she wanted Jen to talk with a counselor.

• • •

Jen is a good example of this large group of people whom we have come to know well in our offices, people whose drinking emerges as a factor in their presenting problems. She did *not* make an appointment with a counselor because she was worried about her drinking. Neither had Dan made any connection between his wife's sleep problem, fatigue, and lack of interest in sex with her drinking (at least not so far).

Was Jen an alcoholic? No. She would not have enough of the symptoms to meet the accepted criteria for any of the alcohol-related diagnoses. She was not someone for whom one drink was never enough. Nor did she drink frequently enough to maintain a certain level of alcohol in her body. She'd never experienced a blackout. And so on. Yet she was clearly experiencing symptoms—such as disturbed sleep, chronic fatigue, depression, and outbursts of anger—that true alcoholics also often report. The answer, for Jen, was that at some point she had crossed over the line that separates normal social drinking from almost alcoholic drinking. The good news, for her, was that this discovery became an opportunity to reassess her drinking (along with the stress that appeared to be driving it) and make some decisions. In the end, she made some changes not only about her drinking, but also about how to cope with the stresses she faced and how to create some balance in her life. She'd had that balance once, as a college student and as a newlywed, but it had gotten uneven as her life became packed with more and more responsibilities.

Let's look at a second example.

Marcus's Story

Marcus, nineteen, had done well in high school despite struggling with attention deficit hyperactivity disorder (ADHD). He'd avoided alcohol during those years—he'd been warned that his ADHD medication didn't mix well with liquor—but once he got to college, he began drinking, usually in binges and in the company of friends.

At first, the downside of Marcus's drinking was fairly subtle: his grades slipped a bit and he sometimes missed classes the morning after drinking. On the upside, he became more outgoing when he drank and was less shy than he'd been through his high school years. A complicating factor for Marcus's situation was his age: drinking in the college-age population typically involves a great deal of binge drinking, which is often organized around drinking games. (*Binge drinking* is defined by the National Institute of Alcohol Abuse and Alcoholism as a drinking pattern corresponding to five or more drinks for a male and four or more for a female within about two hours, resulting in a blood alcohol level of .08 percent or more.) One such game is "beer pong" in which opponents try to bounce a Ping-Pong ball into one another's full glass of beer. When your opponent lands his (or her) ball in your beer, you have to drink it all. Then another round begins.

Marcus found games like beer pong fun. It was socially acceptable and an easy way for him to overcome his shyness. Being drunk also made it easier for him to talk to girls, which further reinforced his behavior.

By the middle of his second semester at school, though, Marcus was in danger of flunking one course and was barely passing three others. To make matters worse, after drinking way too much one Friday night at a fraternity party, he got into a fight with a guy who thought Marcus was flirting with his girlfriend. Words were exchanged, but instead of it ending there, Marcus shoved the guy and then punches were thrown. Fearing it could lead to a brawl, someone dialed 911 for the campus police.

In accordance with the college's zero-tolerance policy

toward violence on campus, Marcus was barred from living on campus the following semester. While he did manage to avoid flunking out, he finished that first year with a grade-point average that jeopardized his chances of getting into the pharmacy school he'd always dreamed of attending.

• • •

Marcus is another example of someone who has crossed the line and entered the gray area of almost alcoholic drinking. Did this young man see the connection between the negative consequences he was experiencing and his drinking behavior? No. The only reason he sought counseling was because, in lieu of a suspension for the rest of that semester, Marcus was offered the option of enrolling in an anger management program at the student counseling center. This is a typical intervention, and not at all unique to Marcus. As we have learned, it is common for authorities (and even loved ones) to focus on a single incident—in Marcus's case, his aggressive behavior—and to identify it as the problem, while ignoring the context (binge drinking) in which it had occurred. This is more evidence that almost alcoholics have until now remained a largely invisible segment of the population.

Research consistently shows that people tend to drink the heaviest in their late teens and early- to mid-twenties. Young adults, both male and female, are especially likely to binge drink. For some of these youths, such drinking may lead to other serious problems. For example, some studies have shown that a region in the brain associated with learning and memory—the hippocampus—is smaller in people who began drinking as adolescents. And studies of teens who were treated for alcohol withdrawal showed that they were more likely to have memory problems than adolescents who did not drink.[2]

Unfortunately, what some college students consider social drinking may include various binge-drinking "games." Not every college student binge drinks, but this behavior tends to be fairly widespread and relatively tolerated by peers on college campuses. It is not uncommon for students to get drunk to the point of passing out. Because of that social context, and also because his drinking was mostly limited to weekends, Marcus viewed his own drinking as normal. He thought he was just doing what a lot of other students did, so how could he have a drinking problem? The reality is that most college students who binge on alcohol will pass through this phase and emerge in adulthood as normal social drinkers. Some of the heaviest drinkers may suffer some memory or learning problems connected to their earlier alcohol use, although they may never make this connection themselves. A few will go on to become full-blown alcoholics. And some, like Marcus, will become almost alcoholics.

Marcus's experiences—getting into a fight and struggling with academics—were clearly consequences of his drinking, yet by themselves they would not have qualified him for a diagnosis of alcoholism. In other words, he didn't fit into the accepted diagnostic "box." Marcus was a client of Dr. Doyle, and it's important to note that if Dr. Doyle had completely cleared Marcus of having a drinking problem, that young man could well have concluded that the negative things that were happening to him were just a matter of bad luck—being in the wrong place at the wrong time—and decide that there was no need to change his drinking behavior. Things could well have continued to go downhill from there. However, by talking about that larger group of people who lie "below the waterline" in terms of their drinking, and by introducing Marcus to the concept of the almost alcoholic, Dr. Doyle was able to open the door that allowed Marcus to see the connection between his drinking and its consequences. From there they could discuss whether Marcus ought to consider doing something about his drinking, even if he was not an alcoholic.

True Alcoholism

Although two physicians, Scotsman Thomas Trotter and American Benjamin Rush, had first talked about alcoholism as a medical condition in the early nineteenth century, it wasn't until the book *Alcoholics Anonymous* was published in 1939 that the idea that alcoholism was a disease with both physical and mental causes began to take hold. It took until 1956 for the American Medical Association to recognize alcoholism as a disease with biological and environmental factors. Until then—and still all too often today—the loss of control that is characteristic of alcoholic drinking was seen as a moral failing or a weakness of will rather than a symptom of a chronic but treatable disease. Today, in its *Diagnostic and Statistical Manual of Mental Disorders (DSM-IV-TR)*, the American Psychiatric Association recognizes alcohol abuse and dependence as disorders with genetic, neurological, and environmental factors.[3]

What are the criteria for being officially diagnosed as an alcoholic? The outset of this chapter offered something of a litmus test. Alcoholics, for example, can't stop drinking once they start. But there are also more detailed answers to the question that are worth looking at. These answers can help us better understand what separates the alcoholic from the almost alcoholic.

The following are symptoms that professionals have considered to be classic indications of alcoholism. The source of this information is the National Institute of Alcohol Abuse and Alcoholism, whose website is a valuable resource: www.niaaa.nih.gov.[4]

- *Craving.* This means just what it says—a strong need, or urge, to drink. The urge to have a drink is never far from consciousness, and alcoholics may become impatient or irritable when they don't have access to alcohol.

- *Tolerance.* This refers to a tendency to need to drink more and more alcohol over time to get the same effect. For example, when an alcoholic first starts out drinking, he or she may feel "tipsy" or "relaxed" after only two drinks. After drinking steadily for a couple of years, it may take four or five drinks to reach that same point of relaxation. This person is said to have developed a "tolerance" for alcohol. Ironically, some people take pride in their ability to "hold their liquor," meaning they can drink a great deal without passing out or falling down. They may take pride in being "the last man (or woman) standing" at a party, but in truth their disease is progressing and is probably already damaging their bodies.

- *Withdrawal.* This refers to symptoms that people in the more advanced stages of alcoholism experience when they totally *stop* drinking alcohol. These symptoms include sweating, a racing pulse, hand tremors, nausea and vomiting, anxiety, insomnia, and possibly seizures and delirium tremens (DTs), which can be fatal. An alcoholic in an advanced stage of the disease has to drink enough so that his or her body is never completely alcohol-free to avoid some or all of these severe and potentially life-threatening withdrawal symptoms, depending on the stage of their disease.

- *Inability to control or stop use.* Alcoholics are engaged in a prolonged and losing inner battle to limit their drinking. Some techniques they try might include drinking wine or beer instead of hard liquor, drinking only on weekends, or having only one cocktail before dinner. Every time they attempt to impose such a rule on themselves, however, they soon break it.

In addition to the aforementioned formal criteria that are used to diagnose an alcoholic, professionals often look for the following telltale signs:

- *Being preoccupied with drinking.* The person may start thinking about having that pre-dinner cocktail around lunchtime. He or she typically worries that the supply of liquor may be running low and makes sure to buy extra. Often, he or she hides an "emergency" bottle to avoid going without a drink.
- *Giving up other activities.* True alcoholics would rather drink than do just about anything else. This means they are likely to turn down invitations for events where liquor will not be available. Most will spend less and less time with nondrinking friends and gradually narrow their social sphere and range of interests. Alcohol becomes their best friend, pushing aside other friends and even lovers.

Below are the current official criteria (symptoms) published by the American Psychiatric Association in its diagnostic manual (*DSM-IV-TR*) that are used to diagnose a person as being "substance dependent," or in this case, an alcoholic. To qualify for that diagnosis, a person must have manifested *three or more* of these symptoms in a twelve-month period:

- Tolerance: a need for markedly increased amounts of alcohol to achieve intoxication or the desired effect, *or* markedly diminished effect with continued use of the same amount of alcohol.
- Withdrawal: physical symptoms such as sweating, diarrhea, etc., *or* using another substance (tranquilizers, etc.) in an effort to avoid withdrawal.
- Drinking in larger amounts *or* over a longer period of time than was intended.
- A persistent desire *or* unsuccessful efforts to cut down or control drinking.
- Preoccupation: a great deal of time and effort is spent obtaining alcohol and maintaining a supply, including possible hidden supplies.
- Important social, occupational, and/or recreational activities are given up or reduced in favor of drinking.
- Drinking continues despite the knowledge of having a persistent or recurrent physical or psychological problem that is likely to have been caused or exacerbated by drinking (diabetes, hypertension, etc.).

A second diagnostic category, alcohol abuse, is recognized by the *DSM-IV-TR* when the following occur within a twelve-month period, but without the other criteria for dependence, e.g., tolerance, withdrawal, and compulsive behavior:

- Recurrent alcohol use resulting in failure to fulfill major role obligations, e.g., repeated absences, suspensions or expulsions from school or work, neglect of children or household, etc.
- Recurrent use in situations that are physically hazardous, e.g., driving, operating machinery, etc.
- Recurrent legal problems related to drinking.
- Continued use despite persistent or recurrent social or interpersonal problems.

Since alcohol abuse has specific diagnostic criteria but does not meet the criteria for alcoholism, we see it as having its own subcategory at the extreme end of the severity range of almost alcoholism.

Now, let's look at Jen and Marcus in light of the criteria used to diagnose alcoholism. Despite Jen's regular consumption of wine, and despite Marcus's binge drinking at weekend parties, neither had yet developed much tolerance for alcohol. Jen had been drinking three glasses of wine a night for years, and Marcus didn't drink other than his binges at parties. Also, when they were sober, neither experienced any withdrawal symptoms. They did not suffer from any physical or psychological problems that they could connect to drinking, nor did their lives revolve around drinking. Neither had been unsuccessful stopping drinking, simply because it had never occurred to either of them to do so. So we might answer "don't know" to the question of whether either of these individuals could stop drinking for a period of time, if they made that decision.

As for being preoccupied with drinking, Jen admitted that she looked forward to her wine at night. On the other hand, she did not think about it during her lunch break or drive home faster so she could have that first drink—both of which are common experiences for alcoholics. In other words, she didn't really *crave* alcohol. Marcus, meanwhile, did not really think about drinking or look forward to it with anticipation. Rather, heavy drinking was simply part of the weekend social scene he was accustomed to. Also, neither he nor Jen had given up friends or activities in order to drink, nor had they hidden a stash of liquor away in case they ran out. Finally, with the exception of Marcus not meeting role obligations, neither he nor Jen had the recurrent problems that define alcohol abuse. The bottom line, then, is that using the official criteria, a professional asked to assess Marcus or Jen would have to conclude that, although both were drinking above low-risk levels, neither was an alcoholic. Such a pronouncement could, in turn, very well lead both of them to conclude that they did not have to consider changing their drinking behaviors. The question is whether such a decision would be in their best long-term interests.

Almost Alcoholic: Five Key Signs

Although Jen and Marcus, like every other almost alcoholic we have worked with, may not have met the required number of the official diagnostic criteria to qualify them as alcoholics, their drinking was marked by five key signs that they were almost alcoholics:

1. You continue drinking despite at least some negative consequences.
2. You look forward to drinking.
3. You drink alone.
4. You sometimes drink to control emotional and/or physical symptoms.
5. You and your loved ones are suffering as a result of your drinking.

Let's examine each of these signs in more detail.

1. You continue drinking despite at least some negative consequences.

This first sign we have discovered is shared by true alcoholics *and* those who drink more than they should but not enough to be considered an alcoholic. In fact, this is the hallmark of the criteria for alcohol abuse in the American Psychiatric Association's *DSM-IV*, where negative consequences are defined as affecting work, family, legal status, physical safety, and social life.

Take our real estate developer, Geraldo, for example. True, he would probably not be diagnosed as alcoholic. But was drinking causing problems for him? Yes it was, both at home and in his work. And what about Marcus? As a college student given to hard partying, he also would not meet all of the criteria to be considered an alcoholic. Yet he's still in trouble, and the connection between his troubles and his drinking is clear, at least when viewed from an objective perspective. If his drinking continues at its current pace, he is likely to experience even more serious consequences and might eventually find that he is among the estimated 10 to 12 percent of the US population who meet the criteria needed to be diagnosed as alcohol dependent. The question is, should Marcus wait until he receives such a diagnosis before seeking help? Because that wait could scuttle his future. For an almost alcoholic, even a short delay can cause long-term problems.

Now let's look at Jen. She's been a steady drinker for years. She does not always drink until she gets drunk; rather, she usually stops after three glasses. Yet three glasses a night, every night for years, can lead to physical harm. One common effect can be a gradual disruption of what is called our "sleep architecture," or the various cycles our sleep goes through. There is, for example, rapid eye movement (REM) sleep, so named because our eyelids tend to move rapidly when we are sleeping at this level. We also dream during REM sleep. From REM sleep, we move to other levels, culminating in so-called deep sleep. It is during this deep sleep that our brains "cleanse" themselves, allowing us to wake the next morning feeling refreshed.

When Jen first started drinking, she may, as she claimed, have felt that it helped her unwind and relax after a long day of work and parenting. Yet by the time she went to her doctor seeking relief from chronic insomnia and fatigue, her sleep architecture had very likely been altered by her years of drinking.[5] One sign of this was the way that Jen described her sleep: she said often fell asleep quickly, only to wake up in the wee hours of the morning, unable to get back to sleep. Most likely, she was not getting nearly enough deep sleep, and that was driving her fatigue, as well as the low-grade depression she complained of.

Although we can't say that Jen was an alcoholic according to the official criteria, was she an almost alcoholic? According to our first critical criterion, the answer would be an unequivocal yes. Like Marcus, Jen may not be able to (or want to) see the connection between her daily drinking and its consequences for her mental health. But the connection, viewed from the outside, is clear. Before they are willing to accept help, people like Jen and Marcus need to understand that they may not be alcoholics, but they are not normal social drinkers either.

2. You look forward to drinking.

With respect to this second key sign, both Marcus and Jen qualify as almost alcoholics. Although Marcus's drinking was mostly limited to parties, he readily admitted that he looked forward to it. He even eagerly anticipated getting drunk. Meanwhile, Jen said she definitely looked forward to her glasses of wine and would have been considerably put out if someone had told her she could not have them.

The next two signs may not be present in every almost alcoholic, but in our experience one or both often are.

3. You drink alone.

The vast majority of people who drink begin their drinking careers in a social context. And for many people, drinking remains largely a social activity throughout their lives. When a person's drinking moves beyond a social setting—when it becomes more than just a social activity and is done alone for its own sake, that is, for the intoxicating effects of alcohol—there is a good chance that he or she has crossed the line separating normal social drinking from the territory we've labeled almost alcoholic. Drinking alone is also common among alcoholics, and whether this behavior indicates that someone has ventured beyond the large gray area of almost alcoholic drinking to alcoholic drinking depends on whether a person meets the criteria for alcohol dependence.

One group that is at increasing risk for alcoholism is older people and the widowed. Not surprisingly, this group is also at risk for social isolation—and social isolation and drinking can go hand in hand.

That was certainly true for Betsy, whose husband, Brad, died a few years ago following a yearlong battle with colon cancer. Married fifty-two years, the couple had raised two sons, both of whom had their own families now, and both of whom lived many hours and many miles away.

Despite being invited by both sons to do so, Betsy had decided against selling the house and moving closer to her family. She did have a circle of friends, she told her sons, and in addition she did not relish the idea of cleaning out her possessions, leaving the house she and Brad had lived in for most of their married lives, and adjusting to a new community.

So Betsy stayed in the house, in the company of a cat she decided to adopt from a woman in her church. She found "George" to be a good companion. She also made a point of going to church every week and continuing with a book club she'd been part of for many years. Despite all of these things, Betsy admitted she often felt lonely. After a few years of living on her own, she realized that although her own health was holding up well, some of her closest friends were less fortunate. The net result was that her social life slowly but steadily dwindled. And as her social life faded away, Betsy's drinking increased. Whereas she once drank only at social occasions, she found that a brandy or two at night helped, in her words "to settle my nerves."

Betsy was drinking to compensate for her loneliness. The amount of brandy she drank slowly increased until two events happened. First, her oldest son asked, during their weekly phone call, if Betsy had been drinking. He politely but firmly pointed out that she was slurring her words. Embarrassed, Betsy replied that she'd had "a couple" of brandies that day, as the weather was cold and she'd felt a chill. In truth, she'd downed five brandies over the course of a Sunday afternoon.

About a month later, Betsy walked down her driveway to fetch the newspaper. On the way back, she tripped and fell, bruising her leg. The pain was bad enough that she decided to drive to the local emergency room. While she was there, awaiting the results of a CT scan, the doctor asked her how much she'd been drinking that afternoon. Again, Betsy was embarrassed, this time even more so because the doctor told her he was sure she was intoxicated and that, even if her leg was fine, he would not allow her to drive herself home. Humiliated, Betsy was forced to call a church friend, who came and drove her home.

Betsy is an example of someone whose drinking behavior included two of the first three critical signs of being an almost alcoholic: She had continued to drink despite at least one clear negative consequence—that phone conversation with her son. Moreover, she had developed a habit of drinking alone.

Betsy's drinking behavior also included our fourth key sign of being an almost alcoholic—drinking to control her emotions, and without intervention, she could have progressed to full alcoholic drinking.

4. You sometimes drink in order to control emotional and/or physical symptoms.

Clearly, Betsy drank to compensate for loneliness. Indeed, almost alcoholics often drink for many reasons that have to do with emotional discomfort, such as

- to relieve stress or "unwind"
- to drown out grief or anxiety
- to overcome social shyness
- to try to overcome insomnia
- to relieve boredom
- to control pain or other physical discomfort

5. You and your loved ones are suffering as a result of your drinking.

The suffering caused by almost alcoholic drinking is often more subtle than that of full-blown alcoholism, but it nonetheless exists. Because the process by which a person becomes an almost alcoholic is so insidious, the suffering is also insidious. It can be years before the connection between drinking and the suffering is made—if it is ever made. In every case we've discussed so far, however, it is easy to see this connection when viewed in terms of being almost alcoholic. And it is not just almost alcoholics who suffer, but their loved ones as well.

The Drinking World: A Spectrum

We have learned over time and through experience that when talking about almost alcoholics, it is often less helpful to talk about formal and official diagnostic criteria for alcoholism—the diagnostic "box" that represents the tip of an iceberg representing all drinkers—and is better to focus instead on these five key indicators that a man or woman is an almost alcoholic. To determine whether this is you (or someone you love), answer these questions:

1. Do you continue to drink despite one or more negative consequences associated with drinking?
2. Do you look forward to drinking?
3. Do you drink alone, and not just socially?
4. Do you sometimes drink to control some emotion?
5. Is your drinking causing suffering for you or a loved one?

These questions are related to the formal diagnostic criteria for alcoholism; they are on the same *spectrum*—only a bit further away from true alcoholism in terms of severity. Those who answer yes to these questions may not have yet suffered the more serious consequences of drinking, or if they have, they are not aware of the connection between their drinking and negative consequences. On the other hand, they have definitely moved beyond normal social drinking.

We have come to view the world of drinkers as not sharply divided into two types of people, but rather as consisting of a wide diversity of people. From our perspective the world looks something like this:

The Drinking World

The critical difference between the way we see the drinking world and the traditional view of alcoholism is shown by the shading from white to a gray that grows darker until it becomes black, creating the three areas, or zones, in this graphic. The large gray area (where Geraldo is now) separates the white zone of what we would call normal social drinking from the black zone of true alcoholism (where Geraldo is not, or at least not yet). The same would apply to all the other cases we've described so far. At any point in time, any one of us who drinks occupies a place somewhere within one of these three zones.

From Low-Risk to Harmful Drinking

Mark Willenbring, MD, former director of the Division of Treatment and Recovery Research at NIAAA, proposed a similar drinking continuum in the American Society of Addiction Medicine's *Principles of Addiction Medicine*, 4th edition.[6] As in our spectrum, Willenbring's includes social drinking (what he calls "low-risk drinking") and dependent drinking on either end of the spectrum. He breaks down what we're calling alcoholic drinking into two categories, which he terms "heavy drinking": at-risk drinking (heavy drinking that doesn't meet the criteria for a diagnosis of abuse or dependence according to the *DSM-IV*) and "harmful drinking," or alcohol abuse.

***DSM-IV-TR* Criteria: Alcohol Abuse (one or more criteria for over a year)**

- Role impairment (e.g., failed work or home obligations)
- Hazardous use, (e.g., driving, swimming, or operating machinery while intoxicated)
- Legal problems related to alcohol use
- Social or interpersonal problems due to alcohol

Source: *Diagnostic and Statistical Manual of Mental Disorders* (4th ed., text rev.), Washington, DC: American Psychiatric Association, 2000.

As we'll see in the next chapter, the diagnostic category of alcohol abuse is a special case of almost alcoholism that falls somewhere toward the far end of the gray zone, but before the full criteria for alcoholism come into play.

Finally, with the possible exception of those whose drinking places them at the extreme right of the alcoholic zone, research has taught us that many people, including some who meet the criteria for alcohol abuse, have the ability to "shift left" and drink less or abstain altogether. Essentially, there is the opportunity to move from one zone to another. However, for the true alcoholic, for whom controlled drinking is by definition almost always unsuccessful, it's commonly accepted that total abstinence, maintained by a personal program of recovery, is the best choice.

2

Becoming an Almost Alcoholic

No one starts drinking with the intention of becoming an alcoholic—or even an almost alcoholic. Surely no one is eager to admit to losing their ability to control their drinking (the alcoholic) or even to see the connection between drinking and its negative consequences (the almost alcoholic). Yet both happen. According to the National Institute on Alcohol Abuse and Alcoholism, approximately 14 percent of people living in the United States have been alcohol dependent at some time in their lives, and about 7 percent are alcohol dependent at any given time.[7] We believe that there are many more people—nationwide and worldwide—who qualify as almost alcoholics.

If asked, most almost alcoholics would deny they have a problem. They would not see the five telltale signs that we are using to characterize almost alcoholic drinking as a problem:

1. Continued drinking despite some negative consequences
2. Looking forward to drinking

3. Drinking alone
4. Drinking to influence emotions or mood
5. Suffering as a result of drinking

In terms of the worldview we presented at the end of the last chapter, the almost alcoholic's drinking might correspond to almost any point in the gray area in the chart below.

The Drinking World

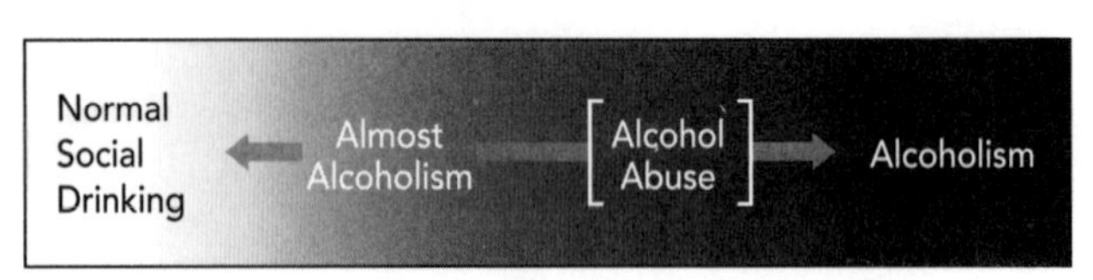

Where Do You Fit in the Drinking World?

In addition to the five most common signs of being almost alcoholic, taking the following quiz can help you identify where your drinking places you along this spectrum in the drinking world. This quiz was devised by researchers to help identify people whose drinking does not qualify them for a diagnosis as an alcoholic but whose drinking is nevertheless a problem worthy of attention.[8]

Take out a pen or pencil and some blank paper (or open up new document in your computer's word processing program) and start a journal where you can explore some of the questions and ideas we'll be raising here and in the following chapters. This is your personal journal and need not be shared with anyone, unless you choose to do so.

To take this quiz, answer each question as it applies to you. Then add the numbers that correspond to your answers to find your score.

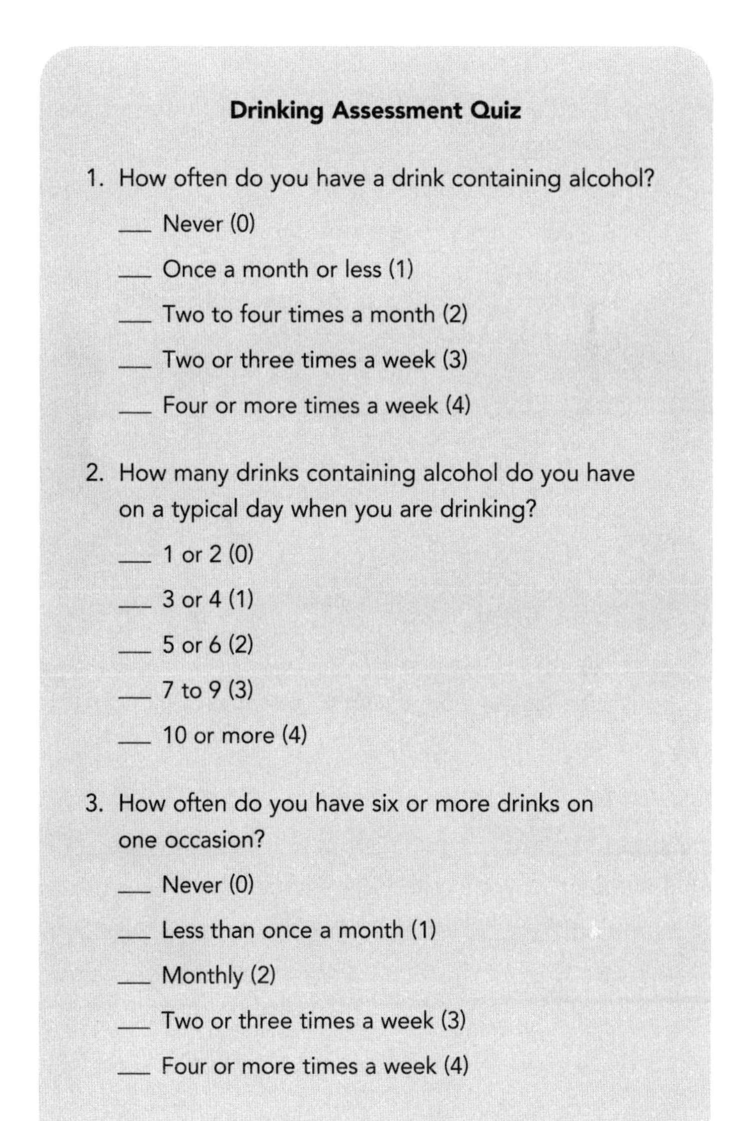

Drinking Assessment Quiz

1. How often do you have a drink containing alcohol?
   ___ Never (0)
   ___ Once a month or less (1)
   ___ Two to four times a month (2)
   ___ Two or three times a week (3)
   ___ Four or more times a week (4)

2. How many drinks containing alcohol do you have on a typical day when you are drinking?
   ___ 1 or 2 (0)
   ___ 3 or 4 (1)
   ___ 5 or 6 (2)
   ___ 7 to 9 (3)
   ___ 10 or more (4)

3. How often do you have six or more drinks on one occasion?
   ___ Never (0)
   ___ Less than once a month (1)
   ___ Monthly (2)
   ___ Two or three times a week (3)
   ___ Four or more times a week (4)

QUIZ CONTINUED ON NEXT PAGE

4. How often during the last year have you found that you were not able to stop drinking once you had started?

    ___ Never (0)

    ___ Less than once a month (1)

    ___ Monthly (2)

    ___ Two or three times a week (3)

    ___ Four or more times a week (4)

5. How often during the last year have you failed to do what was normally expected from you because of drinking?

    ___ Never (0)

    ___ Less than once a month (1)

    ___ Monthly (2)

    ___ Two or three times a week (3)

    ___ Four or more times a week (4)

6. How often during the last year have you needed a first drink in the morning to get yourself going after a heavy drinking session?

    ___ Never (0)

    ___ Less than once a month (1)

    ___ Monthly (2)

    ___ Two or three times a week (3)

    ___ Four or more times a week (4)

7. How often during the last year have you had a feeling of guilt or remorse after drinking?

    ___ Never (0)

QUIZ CONTINUED ON NEXT PAGE

___ Less than once a month (1)

___ Monthly (2)

___ Two or three times a week (3)

___ Four or more times a week (4)

8. How often during the last year have you been unable to remember what happened the night before because you had been drinking?

   ___ Never (0)

   ___ Less than once a month (1)

   ___ Monthly (2)

   ___ Two or three times a week (3)

   ___ Four or more times a week (4)

9. Have you or someone else been injured as a result of your drinking?

   ___ No (0)

   ___ Yes, but not in the last year (2)

   ___ Yes, during the last year (4)

10. Has a relative, a friend, a doctor, or another health care worker expressed concern about your drinking and suggest you cut down?

    ___ No (0)

    ___ Yes, but not in the last year (2)

    ___ Yes, during the last year (4)

YOUR TOTAL SCORE: ___________

If we think of drinking as existing along a spectrum that includes the gray zone of almost alcoholic drinking which falls between the two most commonly recognized categories—social drinking and alcoholism—it's easy to see how your score on the quiz can place you somewhere in our diagram of the drinking world. Naturally, those who do not drink at all would not occupy a place on this spectrum. Normal social drinkers include those with scores no higher than 8. From there we enter that zone that lies between normal social drinking and alcoholism. That zone is fairly wide—in other words, not all almost alcoholics are the same. However, the further into the zone a person goes, the more likely he or she will begin to show symptoms associated with alcohol dependence. Scores of 30 or higher certainly place a person at risk for these symptoms.

Making the Connection

Viewed through the eyes of the almost alcoholic, though, life does not seem so bad. When we see them in our offices—again, usually for a problem other than drinking—and if we ask about their drinking behavior, the most common response we get is "No problem." Yet there is a problem. Their lives *are* being affected by drinking; they just don't see the connection between negative experiences in their lives and their drinking behavior. Other people in their lives, however, may see the connection sooner or later.

For example, when Kurt went to see a therapist for his alleged "depression," he was asked about how often and how much he drank. Kurt tried to soft-pedal it. "I like a beer or two," was his reply. On hearing this, Kurt's wife, Stacy, squirmed visibly in her chair. "You seem uncomfortable, Stacy," the therapist said to her. "Why is that?"

Stacy paused, looked over at Kurt, and then let it out: "You mean you *used to* like a couple of beers. Do you realize that for at least the past five years, you down at least three, sometimes four beers a night—and that on the weekends you can finish off more than a six-pack a day? Do you realize how much money you spend on liquor? Are you aware that you pretty much pass out every night at nine, while I spend the next couple of hours alone, watching television until I'm tired enough to go to sleep?"

Kurt blushed. Then the therapist followed up. "Kurt," he asked, "you've said that you feel 'depressed.' The symptoms you've described include feeling down, not having much energy, letting things go around the house, and losing your motivation at work. Those things can also be the result of drinking as much as you do, on a steady basis and for years. Now, you may not be an alcoholic, but I think Stacy has a point. There probably is a connection between your drinking and the issues that brought you here."

• • •

As Kurt's case illustrates, almost alcoholics *are* suffering. In some cases (depending on where they are in our spectrum of the drinking world), they may be suffering as much as full-blown alcoholics. Moreover, their suffering spills over into their lives as a whole, affecting those closest to them. All of the cases we've discussed so far illustrate how being an almost alcoholic affects a person on many levels: as a spouse, as a parent, and as an employee.

Today, most doctor visits are limited to a matter of minutes, which leaves little time to connect any potential dots between drinking and its consequences. Meanwhile, professionals such as psychologists, psychiatrists, and social workers must be able to support a diagnosis of full-blown alcoholism in order to justify treatment that would be covered by insurance. If clinicians are required to identify and treat only those people who meet the full criteria for a psychiatric disorder, including alcoholism, they have virtually no time or resources to explore and help people with not-so-obvious problems that don't appear to pose any immediate health threat—people like the millions of almost alcoholics out there.

Almost alcoholics often react with confusion, hurt, or anger if it's suggested that drinking may be a problem for them. This is understandable since drinking is considered a normal social activity; to have a "problem" with drinking, therefore, amounts to saying you aren't normal. Some people also feel threatened by the prospect. It is also true that just having the comfort taken away—the "medicating" effects that alcohol brings for some people—can be seen as a threat.

Almost alcoholics readily admit that they drink—but they will quickly add that so does everyone they know. Like Geraldo, Jen, Marcus, and Kurt, they may also admit that they enjoy drinking and claim that it relaxes them—but they don't drink compulsively, they argue. Privately, though, many almost alcoholics have told us that they did have concerns, at least at times, about their own drinking, and that they only became defensive when someone else brought it up. Here is an example.

"It was like my cover was blown," Shirley said. "I did not think for one minute that I was an alcoholic. My father had been an alcoholic, and my brother is one. I know what that is like, and it wasn't me. But I also knew that I like my drinks, and was aware that the older I got the more quickly I got tired at night after a couple of drinks. I didn't like to think about that, though. But when my husband pointed it out and said that he wished I would drink less so I could stay up longer and be with him, that hit home. I felt exposed, and my first reaction was to get angry. After I thought about it, though, I had to admit he had a point."

Diagnostic Orphans

The medical literature has a term for almost alcoholics; they are called "diagnostic orphans"—that is, their problems don't fit neatly into established diagnostic categories. This means that if they went to a professional for an assessment, they wouldn't fit the criteria for the diagnosis of alcohol dependence. People may also be diagnostic orphans when it comes to other problems. For example, a mild but persistent and debilitating depression may not meet all the criteria for any of the various diagnostic categories for depression. Thus, "almost depression" may be overlooked, just as almost alcoholic drinking often is—even though this person is suffering, just as the almost alcoholic is suffering. When that happens, people really need help but may fall through the cracks in the medical/mental health system.

Ironically, many almost alcoholics do get treatment, but not for the real cause of their problems. They may seek help for problems such as depression, sleep problems, temper issues, or for other health problems such as hypertension or diabetes. If they are lucky, their almost alcoholic behavior will not lead to deeper trouble. But the key word is *lucky*. For many almost alcoholics, luck eventually runs out.

Fortunately, despite the complications caused by being a diagnostic orphan, we have found that almost alcoholics can nevertheless gain insight into their situation and, drawing on that insight, can make a "course correction" in their lives. The change doesn't necessarily have to be dramatic; sometimes even a small adjustment can be enough to mitigate the most harmful consequences of almost alcoholic drinking. Here's an example.

Aubrey's Story

Aubrey, now thirty-five, was always the life of the party in college. She smoked marijuana most weekends. Plus, like some of her peers, she'd discovered that psycho-stimulants, which are commonly used to treat attention deficit disorder (and which she obtained without a prescription, from friends), helped her concentrate when she needed to cram for exams. This was true even though she did not have attention deficit disorder.

Aubrey avoided drugs she considered to be "dangerous," such as heroin and cocaine. She believed alcohol was not nearly as dangerous as the illicit drugs she saw others use, or even the pot she liked to smoke because it helped her "chill."

Like her siblings, Aubrey was one of those people who could drink a lot and not seem—at least from the outside—to be drunk. Even so, there had been a few times when she'd had a lot to drink and the next morning could not remember what she'd done the night before. But she just wrote off these few experiences (which were actually blackouts) to chance.

After graduating college, Aubrey returned to the semi-rural community she'd grown up in, where she looked up her high school sweetheart who still lived there. They started dating and two years later they married. Soon thereafter, Aubrey became pregnant with her first child, a daughter.

The family soon expanded again with a second child. Although Aubrey put her pot-smoking days behind her upon becoming pregnant the first time, and she drank only rarely (and very little) during her two pregnancies, Aubrey described alcohol as being a "part of life" in her native southern Louisiana. She loved getting together with her girlfriends for cocktails and "clubbing." She also liked hiring a babysitter and then hanging out with her husband at a sports bar, watching a big game, and downing a few beers. She was a stay-at-home mother, and these activities helped to counteract the loneliness and stress of her days with her two preschool children. In the afternoon, when they were napping, she liked to drink wine while she read a book or watched the news.

Then one night after a night out with two girlfriends, Aubrey was driving home in the rain and took a sharp turn going much too fast. Her car skidded, turned sideways, and narrowly missed an oncoming car as it slid off the road and landed in a culvert, where it got stuck. Though unhurt, Aubrey was clearly shaken.

Aubrey called 911 and soon the police were on the scene. It being a small town, the reporting trooper knew Aubrey, the driver of the other car, and Aubrey's husband. The trooper called for a tow truck; he also called Aubrey's husband. No one asked Aubrey to take a sobriety test, in part because, as usual, she didn't appear to be drunk. The accident was written off to bad weather.

• • •

There is a lesson to be drawn from Aubrey's story: it can be difficult to draw a definitive "line in the sand" that separates a social drinker from an almost alcoholic. It typically comes down to a judgment call. Often, it's only when people close to a drinker perceive a noticeable *change* in a person's behavior or personality, or following one or more severe drinking-related *consequences*, that a red flag will go up in either the drinker's mind or in the mind of someone close to them.

Again, it's not just how many drinks people have that signal almost alcoholic behavior—it's *when* they drink, *who* they drink with, *how their bodies respond* to alcohol, how much *stress* they're under and how they're handling it, and how their drinking affects their personal, academic, and professional lives.

Aubrey had a high tolerance for alcohol—but she'd always been that way, so a *change* here would probably not be noticeable. Also, Aubrey had always liked to drink and did so regularly with friends. Again, no *change* in the frequency of her drinking might be evident to others.

It's not surprising, then, that neither Aubrey, her husband, nor her friends thought of Aubrey as an alcoholic. Similarly, if Aubrey were to see a mental health professional for an assessment of her drinking, the outcome could well confirm that she is not an alcoholic. Yet like Marcus and Jen in the first chapter, Aubrey is arguably in trouble and potentially faces more problems in the future. She is an almost alcoholic who is just lucky (or maybe not so lucky in the long run) to live in a community where she is well known and where drinking is an accepted part of the social scene.

Some of the indications that Aubrey is an almost alcoholic include the following:

- *Drinking to relieve stress.* Aubrey met all five of our critical signs of being an almost alcoholic, beginning with the fact that she drank to control her emotional state. In Aubrey's case, it was to relieve what she described as the stress of being a stay-at-home mother. Although she and her husband agreed that this is what they wanted, Aubrey said that being at home with her children was a "mixed blessing." On the one hand, she appreciated that her husband made enough money to allow her to stay home. She felt that her kids got a lot more quality mothering than the children of many of her friends who were working mothers. On the other hand, she was not utilizing her college education and felt quite bored and frustrated at times. She looked forward to her weekly outings with friends—including the drinking that was involved—as a relief from this stress. This use of alcohol as a stress reliever is very common among almost alcoholics.
- *Drinking alone.* Not only did Aubrey drink to relieve stress and feel good when she saw her friends, but she also had developed a habit of having a glass or two of wine in the afternoon before her husband got home from work.
- *Anticipation.* Aubrey eventually found herself looking forward to having a drink. Although she rarely drank before midafternoon, she began thinking about having that first drink around lunchtime. And sometimes she found herself watching the clock, deliberately holding back until the clock struck three.

- *Negative consequences.* There's no question about it: drinking contributed to Aubrey's accident as much as or more than any weather conditions. And where there is one such negative drinking-related consequence, others are usually not far behind.
- *Caused suffering.* Although Aubrey escaped the legal consequences of her drinking, the embarrassment to her and her husband and the costs of the accident caused suffering. Of course, she and her loved ones would have experienced further emotional pain had she been arrested or, even worse, hurt or killed in the accident.

More Insights from Research

A study of 35,000 people—the National Epidemiologic Survey on Alcohol and Related Conditions (NESARC)—found that people who drink regularly but whose drinking behavior does not meet the criteria for a diagnosis of alcohol dependence report continuing to engage in high-risk behaviors such as drinking and driving. They are also likely to report having issues related to their mental health. For example, as many as 9 percent, or 19 million Americans, who would fall within the middle range of being almost alcoholics suffer from a mood disorder such as depression. Another 11 percent of this group, representing some 23 million adults, suffer from an anxiety disorder.[9] The researchers concluded that these individuals (whom we define as almost alcoholics) would benefit from an intervention. In other words, they need help. Why? Because their condition is likely to persist and can result in significant dysfunction, even if it never progresses to full-blown alcoholism. In addition, the NESARC investigators found that early treatment of an alcohol problem—in other words, helping the almost alcoholic —translated into a 30-percent *decrease* in the risk for major depression. Since depression and anxiety impair a person's job or school performance, present a danger to the person's physical health, and account for the majority of psychiatric medication dispensed in the United States, it makes as much sense to offer help to the almost alcoholic as it does to help an alcoholic.

Almost Alcoholic Behavior

We've already identified the primary signs of being an almost alcoholic: Aubrey, for example, had all five of them. Even so, she had no intention of forgoing future nights out with her friends because of the accident. She did, however, commit to not driving home if she had more than one drink and, not being an alcoholic, she was able to stick to that and avoid future life-threatening accidents.

Over time, we've noticed certain other almost alcoholic behavior patterns. Although these patterns may not be present in every almost alcoholic, people who can identify with one or more of these patterns likely fall somewhere along the spectrum of almost alcoholism. They are also likely to have scores of 10 or more on the Drinking Assessment Quiz. These patterns include the following.

Binge Drinking

Some almost alcoholics drink only occasionally—but when they do drink, they have a tendency to binge. Two glasses of wine with dinner every night is not the same as 14 glasses at a party Saturday night, even though in both instances 2 x 7 = 14. The real issue for binge drinkers, rather, is that once they do start to drink, they usually don't stop until they are drunk.

This pattern described Phil, whose wife, Sarah, was worried for him and for herself. Phil was a teacher, and both he and Sarah acknowledged that if he ever got arrested for driving while intoxicated, he'd likely lose his job. That, in turn, would cause them to lose their home, since the mortgage demanded two full-time incomes. They loved their house and enjoyed gardening, landscaping, and decorating together on weekends.

Phil was a member of a club whose shared passion was classic cars. Phil himself had a vintage Mustang. Like all the other club members, he kept the vehicle garaged in a large, secure, rented barn. The club members met there, year-round, every Wednesday night to fix, polish, or otherwise work on their cars—and also to drink beer and talk about cars.

Phil would always promise Sarah that, if he drank, he'd nurse only a single beer. And indeed, about half the time Phil went to the club, he didn't drink at all. But on those nights when he did drink, Phil could never stop at one. By the time he got home on those nights, it was pretty obvious to Sarah that he was tipsy and had driven home in that condition. Invariably, this would lead to an argument.

Sarah would insist that Phil was an alcoholic and that he should either get treatment or start going to AA. Phil would react defensively and deny that he was an alcoholic, arguing that he just drank a little too much sometimes. The truth lay somewhere in between: Phil did not meet the diagnostic criteria for alcohol dependence; however, one could make a case that he was an almost alcoholic since he knew he was taking a risk by drinking and then driving home and he would repeatedly violate the "one drink" rule anyway. In other words, he continued his drinking behavior despite one or more negative consequences (the ire of his wife and the stress of continuing to do what he knew was dangerous), one of our five criteria for being somewhere in the almost alcoholic zone on our spectrum.

By his own admission, Phil had always been "sensitive" to alcohol—he could get tipsy on two or three beers, whereas his friends seemed better able to "hold their liquor." And Sarah was correct that an arrest would be devastating to both of them. It might take many years (if ever) for Phil's behavior to progress to the point that he would be diagnosed as an alcoholic. But from our perspective, he had already crossed the line from normal social drinking to being an almost alcoholic. The only way we could see that he could return to normal social drinking was to successfully limit himself to one drink. And that would be a challenge for him.

Driving Intoxicated Multiple Times

Almost alcoholics may never have been arrested for driving while intoxicated, but many have driven that way many times.

Robert was a college professor who came to counseling for what he described as a nagging depression and lack of energy. He thought he needed antidepressant medication. During his first few sessions, however, his therapist began to suspect that Robert's problem might stem from his long-standing drinking pattern. If that were true, antidepressants would make no difference.

Initially, Robert was reluctant to talk about his drinking—he didn't see it as a problem. After all, he was a tenured professor with a list of publications as long as his arm. He got high ratings from his students, and he rarely missed a day of work.

He did admit that he enjoyed martinis and had been enjoying them for many years.

Then the therapist casually asked Robert how often, in his opinion, he had driven while intoxicated. Robert quickly replied that he'd never been arrested for driving while intoxicated. "That's not my question," the therapist responded. "I want to know how often you drive after you've had more than one martini." Robert hesitated, then replied in a soft voice, "A lot."

Drinking to Get High

Almost alcoholics may like to maintain a "buzz."

Henry is a successful real estate broker. He inherited the business from his father and grew it. Now one of his own sons and his daughter are also brokers and partners in the family business. At age sixty, Henry is well known in the community, having found over the years that being visible, making friends, entertaining, and giving to local charities is good for business.

Henry also enjoys drinking and drinks pretty much every day. He does not, however, binge drink. Rather, his preference is for expensive bourbon or single malt scotch, which he drinks on the rocks with a splash of water. He never downs a drink quickly, but prefers to sip—and sip, and sip.

Henry "sips" whiskey every day. He's not ashamed to say that he likes "to keep a warm glow," by which he means drinking slowly but continuously from the time he starts until he goes to bed. He then falls soundly asleep, though for the past few years has found that, after waking to go to the bathroom around 3 a.m., he often has trouble getting back to sleep.

For years, Henry has made a habit of buying eight season

tickets for the home football games at the local college. He and his wife, Lorna, load up their large, comfortable recreational vehicle with food and liquor and invite several friends, business acquaintances, or local officials to join them for a tailgate party before the football game. They are hugely popular for doing this.

Last year Lorna spoke with Henry about his drinking after they got home from one of their tailgate parties. She explained that she was worried about him because, although he'd been diagnosed with hypertension and high cholesterol and had been advised by his doctor to limit his alcohol consumption, he continued his habit of keeping a warm glow.

Lorna confronted Henry about how much he drank at the last tailgate party—nearly a third of a bottle of scotch, slowly but steadily, over the course of five or six hours. Henry laughed off his wife's comment. He was an old dog, he said, and he wasn't interested in learning any new tricks.

Again, the question: is Henry an alcoholic? Some might say yes, because it appears he has a need to maintain a blood alcohol level—his "warm glow." On the other hand, he always sobers up the next morning and does not begin "sipping" again until just before dinner.

Surely we'd have a hard time convincing Henry that he is an alcoholic, especially in light of how he responded to his wife's concerns. He could point to his success in business, for example, or to the fact that he's never had a DUI or a drinking-related car accident, as evidence that can "hold his liquor." On the other hand, Henry does have medical problems, his doctor has recommended he cut down on his alcohol consumption, he likes to keep a buzz going most evenings in spite of his doctor's advice and his wife's concerns, and alcohol is likely messing up his "sleep architecture."[10] So even if he is not an alcoholic, a strong case can be made that Henry is an almost alcoholic.

Diminished Performance at Work

Almost alcoholics may get to work every day, but they really aren't on their best game. Earlier we talked about Geraldo, the man who worked in commercial real estate and who, in response to increasing work-related stress caused by a severe economic turndown, had begun to drink more—including when he traveled on business. He still showed up for work every day, but Geraldo was not as sharp the morning after downing several beers, cocktails, or glasses of wine. If this pattern continued, and if his projects failed to meet profit projections, Geraldo could well find himself in trouble. He, too, is an almost alcoholic, living somewhere in that zone between normal social drinking and alcoholism.

Holding Out for a Drink

Are you someone who is able to "hold out" on drinking? Do you, for example, find yourself glancing at your watch, waiting for happy hour to start? Or, when the weekend comes, do you count down to six o'clock, so you can pour yourself that cocktail you've been looking forward to all afternoon? If so, you may have ventured into the almost alcoholic zone.

Unlike normal social drinkers, almost alcoholics often find themselves holding out until they can drink. They may begin to feel impatient the longer they have to wait for that first drink. Although they may not binge, they will most likely crave that drink. The normal social drinker, in contrast, does not experience this kind of craving or the need to deliberately resist it.

Sally's drinking habits qualified her as a holdout. She never drank before 6 p.m. One reason for this "rule" was that her mother had been an alcoholic whom Sally described as "pretty much always half in the bag."

Growing up, Sally had always been amazed that her mother could get to work every day, because she seemed forever hungover and half the time would pass out on the couch at night instead of going to bed. She drank cheap wine, which she bought in gallon-size jugs. And she always made sure to have a spare in the closet, ready to open when her current one ran dry.

When she was fifty-two, Sally's mother was diagnosed with diabetes, and when she was fifty-five, with sclerosis of the liver. Her drinking slowed after that, but as far as Sally knew, it had never stopped completely, and she died at sixty-one.

Sally regarded her mother as an alcoholic, and no doubt she was right. But Sally sees herself as different. She is not, for example, always "half in the bag." She drinks only expensive wine—and she buys standard-size bottles, not gallon bottles (although she does buy it by the case, to save money). And Sally says she can count on one hand the number of times she's had a hangover.

Despite differences like these, Sally is not just a normal social drinker. Starting promptly at 6 p.m. every day, Sally pours herself a glass of wine. During the next two to three hours she drinks two, sometimes three more glasses. She does not consider this to be a problem. She says it helps her "unwind" from her busy day as a dental hygienist. A single mother, she has two children who she tends to without fail, is in excellent health, and rarely misses a day of work. She does admit, however, that she often thinks about having a drink on her way home from work and watches the clock, waiting for 6 p.m. to arrive.

Is Sally an alcoholic? Hard to say, but unless your sole defining criteria is *daily* drinking, she wouldn't meet the criteria for that diagnosis. She does not seem to have built up much of a tolerance, either, because although she drinks every day and has for years, she never has more than three or four glasses of wine at a time. On the other hand, Sally justifies her argument that she does not have a drinking problem by virtue of the fact that she has (so far) been able to stick to her "six o'clock rule" on drinking. Even so, Sally does drink alone, and it's safe to say that she created this rule to put a check on her urge to drink. That's not normal social drinking, and it's possible that in time Sally may find herself breaking her rule.

Medicating Social Anxiety

Almost alcoholics may drink to overcome social anxiety. Like the Indian physicist on the popular TV show *The Big Bang Theory*, they are able to socialize only after first having one or more drinks. Although alcohol does relax them, at least initially, over time two things can happen. First, they may gradually need to drink more to achieve the same "relaxing" effect. In other words, they may gradually build up a tolerance to alcohol. This tolerance tends to sneak up on people, so they are not really aware that they need to drink more now than they did, say two or three years ago, in order to unwind.

Second, they may find themselves prone to feeling depressed. Most of us have known people who say that drinking helps them "lighten up," relieving anxiety and making it easier for them to "climb out of their shell." That's because alcohol is a disinhibitor. It has the potential not only to mask social anxiety, but also to disinhibit all sorts of emotions and behaviors, including depression, anger, and libido (as Ogden Nash famously wrote, "Candy is dandy, but liquor is quicker").

Drinking enables some people who would otherwise avoid social contact to tolerate social situations. If they didn't drink, they say, their social lives would shrivel. At other times, they may not drink much or at all. However, they are in one sense dependent on alcohol—to be social. Here's an example.

Charlie has been drinking to overcome severe social anxiety—which he refers to as his shyness—since he was in high school. Charlie, despite being intelligent and reasonably attractive, has always had low self-esteem, especially around women. In his college years, he drank heavily whenever he was faced with a social situation. It seemed that the only way he could bring himself to even talk to a girl—especially one he thought was attractive—was if he first got drunk.

As a result, although Charlie was able to talk to girls when he drank, many were turned off because he was obviously drunk. The few who responded positively to him were invariably also drunk (and perhaps just as socially anxious). On the few occasions when he had sex, he'd usually pass out soon afterward, only to awaken the next day alone and unable to clearly remember who his partner had been or even what she'd looked like. And he'd never had a steady girlfriend.

Now thirty-four and single, Charlie has friends who would like to "match" him with available single women, for example, by inviting him for dinner or a barbecue. He works as an information technology specialist for a large corporation that does a lot of business with the US Department of Defense. This gives him job security and has an added advantage: it allows him to make a good living without having to interact face to face with people very often. He is quite satisfied interacting with others via e-mail.

Charlie would like to have a girlfriend. In fact, he'd like to get married and have a family. The problem is that he's still socially anxious. Other than for social occasions, Charlie drinks in relative moderation. He might have a glass of cabernet with dinner, but never more than that. He never misses work or shows up hungover, and he's been diligent enough to earn two promotions in three years. On the other hand, he still has to drink to steel himself for social occasions when he knows he'll meet someone. And while he no longer arrives drunk (or gets drunk) at such occasions, Charlie does drink quite a bit, and on a couple of occasions, he's been told afterward that his drinking turned off the woman he'd been there to meet.

So is Charlie (a) an alcoholic, (b) an almost alcoholic, or (c) just a normal social drinker? What do you think? We think he's an almost alcoholic, because he continues to drink even though his drinking leads to negative social consequences—just as it did in his college years. And in all this time, he's never considered an alternative to improving his comfort in social settings, such as seeking counseling to work on his social anxiety and low self-esteem.

• • •

So far we've talked about what an almost alcoholic is and described some of the behaviors and patterns most often associated with being an almost alcoholic. We've also discussed our belief that the world is not simply divided into two kinds of people—alcoholics and nonalcoholics—and we presented a quiz to help you see just where you (and people you know) fit within "the drinking world." In the next chapter we'll look at your relationship to alcohol as one more way to think of drinking as a behavior that exists along a spectrum.

3

Your Relationship with Alcohol

In this chapter we'll examine another way of looking at drinking, and that is in terms of a *relationship* between you and alcohol. Most of the people we counsel are able to relate to this concept and can even name the kind of relationship they have with alcohol. We will look at three potential stages of this relationship: casual friendship, serious relationship, and commitment.

Stage 1: Casual Friendship

People whose relationship with alcohol falls into this stage drink primarily in social settings. This is what we mean by "normal social drinking." It's a glass or two of wine at a wine and cheese get-together among friends, a couple of beers at the Sunday afternoon football party, or an occasional happy hour cocktail with co-workers. If the person does drink alone at this stage of use, it is not typically on a daily basis and involves only a drink or two in one sitting.

Social users never binge, and they are not psychologically "dependent" on drinking, for example, to overcome social anxiety. People have used alcohol socially—indeed, it has been called a "social lubricant"—for centuries. Drinking in this context is said to help people "loosen up" or "relax." And in small quantities, alcohol may do this. A glass of wine or a beer can take the edge off just about any common stress a person may be feeling. It can disinhibit the drinker just a bit (hence the term "unwind") and thereby facilitate social interaction. Although alcohol can affect a person's emotional state even at this first stage, these effects are generally positive, are considered desirable, and tend to fade as the alcohol is metabolized. In other words, the person returns to normal after drinking socially and doesn't usually drink enough to wake up with a hangover the next morning.

Although negative consequences may occur at any stage of drinking, they are relatively rare at this stage. Moreover, at this stage most people's blood alcohol level will remain under the legal limit with one or two drinks and they will be capable of driving in relatively short order, because their bodies are able to metabolize the alcohol fairly efficiently.

Viewed from a relational perspective, at this first stage of use—the social stage—alcohol can be thought of as a *casual friend.* In most cases, neither the drinker nor his or her friends or loved ones perceive alcohol as a problem, much less a threat, to their other relationships. Consequently, at the social stage, alcohol use is most often met with tolerance or acceptance.

Stage 2: Serious Relationship

When we say a casual friendship has progressed to a "serious relationship," we are implying that our connection has grown stronger. So it is with alcohol. In this second stage, a person has learned to use alcohol *consistently* for one of two reasons: to create certain positive feelings (such as relaxation or euphoria) or to avoid certain negative feelings (such as anxiety or loneliness).

This type of drinking falls within the large gray area that we have defined as the *almost alcoholic* zone on the drinking spectrum. The area is indeed "gray." First, there is no sharp line that separates normal social drinking from almost alcoholic drinking. Second, the zone itself includes considerable degrees of drinking, with some people being much closer to true alcoholism than others.

Rather than stepping over a distinct line, a person gradually slips away from social drinking and into the almost alcoholic zone. Eventually, the symptoms and behavior patterns associated with being an almost alcoholic start to appear.

The person who is developing a serious relationship with alcohol is someone who may begin to drink alone as well as socially. This is an important change in drinking behavior because as a person crosses into that gray zone from drinking mainly in social situations to also drinking alone, his or her relationship with alcohol gets serious. It's no longer just a casual friend but is now a reliable "buddy."

Most people who drink at this stage are consistently trying either to achieve certain emotional effects, to allow themselves to engage in certain behaviors, or to overcome negative emotions, such as social anxiety and their consequences (shyness, self-consciousness). As time goes on and drinkers come to rely on their "buddy" alcohol, they may find themselves drinking more consistently (and in larger quantities) than social drinkers. As a result, they are more vulnerable to certain negative consequences, such as more frequent hangovers, unpredictable mood changes, or lack of concentration and mental acuity. In time their bodies become less efficient at metabolizing alcohol, and as a result, they may feel tipsy more quickly. This can lead to behavior that may later embarrass them and can also increase the likelihood that they'll fail a sobriety test—after drinking the same amount that before wouldn't have put them over the limit.

At the serious relationship level, consistent heavy drinking over time—even by men and women who are not true alcoholics—can place people at increased risk for various kinds of cancer. In a "meta-analysis" of 229 studies of cancer in nineteen sites in the body, researchers found that risk increased along with how much a person drank on a daily basis, from none to two, four, or eight drinks a day. The bottom line was this: the more that people drank, the greater their risk for cancer. The areas of the body at highest risk for cancer in those who drank included the upper respiratory tract, liver, colon, rectum, and breast.[11]

How is drinking related to cancer? The most likely explanation is that as alcohol (ethanol) is metabolized in the liver, it produces *acetaldehyde*, a chemical that the International Agency for Research on Cancer has designated as a carcinogen.[12] Choosing to believe that drinking can harm one's health only if and when one reaches the point of becoming alcoholic is clearly foolish.

Despite these realities, it is unusual for drinkers at the serious relationship stage to view themselves as having a drinking problem. For one thing, the connection between increased drinking, or drinking alone, and any negative consequences may be vague at best. An arrest for driving while intoxicated (or at least, a first arrest), for example, may be written off to simple bad luck. And although they are increasing their risk for developing cancer or other health problems, they may have yet to experience any overt physical symptoms.

Significant others, too, are inclined to give drinkers at this level a pass. However, friends, spouses, and others who know them will usually begin to notice the change in how *often* the almost alcoholics drink, how *much* they drink, and how drinking *affects* them. Almost alcoholics may joke to justify their increased drinking ("It's always five o'clock somewhere!" or "The economy is making work a major stress!").

Family members, spouses, and friends may begin to feel a bit uncomfortable about the person's evolving relationship with alcohol. Some have said that they actually felt jealous of this relationship, which they perceived as taking more and more of a center-stage position in the almost alcoholic's life. At the same time, they may hesitate to speak up about this, thinking they are wrong to feel that way or simply wanting to avoid a potential confrontation with the drinker.

Interestingly enough, significant others who were raised in alcoholic homes may fail to react to substance abuse at the serious relationship stage. Instead of being sensitized by their early experiences, the opposite often occurs: they have become *desensitized* through their exposure to excessive drinking and fail to perceive this relationship to alcohol as serious (or a threat). Consequently, they are more likely to react only after drinking has progressed either deeply into the almost alcoholic zone or into alcoholism itself.

Stage 3: Commitment

At this next stage, alcohol use has moved beyond a serious relationship into what could be called a commitment that the drinker has made with alcohol. The title of a book that describes one woman's descent into alcoholism—*Drinking: A Love Story* by the late Caroline Knapp—succinctly captures the essence of this stage.[13] This is the right end of the drinking spectrum, in that gray area that separates being *almost alcoholic* from alcohol abuse and for some, like Knapp, sliding over into true alcoholism. This book vividly depicts the journey of a high-functioning woman who careens from normal social drinking through the almost alcoholic zone and into alcoholism.

Loved ones often can identify with this idea of someone having made a commitment to drinking. By the time drinking has progressed to this stage, they can see how that commitment is not only intimate (like a marriage) but is also one that begins to seriously compete with drinkers' other commitments—to spouses, children, friends, and work.

The committed drinker makes sure that he or she is never far from alcohol. Over time, his or her lifestyle begins to revolve more and more around drinking. One husband described how his wife, as she moved into this stage of drinking, refused to go anywhere that she could not drink. She refused, for example, to take a bus tour with him to visit three national parks because she could not take liquor on the bus. And as one wife put it, "My husband won't go anywhere without his cooler. It's as attached to him as his wedding ring." If that last comment isn't an image of commitment, we don't know what would be!

At the commitment stage, negative consequences linked to

drinking become increasingly apparent, at least to others, and these almost invariably include strained relationships. Decreased effectiveness at work, financial problems, and declining health may also become evident as habitual drinking progresses. The drinker, however, may continue to blame anything *but* alcohol for these consequences. Car accidents, for example, may be attributed to the other driver, defective tires, or poor road conditions. Poor performance evaluations are attributed to a bad boss. Failing health may be attributed to bad luck or to bad genes—and so on.

Finally, definite personality changes begin to appear as a person drifts into the commitment stage. In the emotional sphere, these changes most often include a growing emotional instability, increased aggressiveness and irritability, and depression. Psychologically, the habitual drinker becomes progressively more self-absorbed, unreliable, and demanding—in a word, *childlike*.

At this stage of drinking, significant others become angry and anxious, as well as increasingly frustrated, as their repeated attempts to control the other person's drinking fail. Confrontations over drinking may occur more frequently and come to threaten the stability of relationships with loved ones. If the drinker has slid over into dependency, attempts to control or limit drinking inevitably end in failure. Unless there is a strong pattern of codependency (in which a loved one is *dependent* on controlling the addict's using) and enabling, spouses and children begin to detach from the committed drinker for self-preservation and lead their own separate lives. In short, the committed drinker eventually *alienates* his or her loved ones unless they, too, are committed drinkers or are pathologically codependent.

Once drinking has become a commitment, turning back and returning to normal social drinking is, in our experience, extremely difficult for the person who is in the far right of the almost alcoholic gray area and nearly impossible for the true alcoholic. If a committed drinker does want to turn back, we strongly recommend that he or she begin with an extended period of abstinence—six months at a minimum. The help of a counselor experienced with treating addictions is also essential. But we do not want to be misleading here: turning back from committed drinking to a casual friendship or even a serious relationship with alcohol may not be an option; abstinence may be the only sane choice.

Scott is an example of someone whose relationship with alcohol progressed through all of the above stages. Let's look at his story.

Scott's Story

Now fifty-eight, Scott has been a self-described "heavy drinker" since late adolescence. He drank heavily and continuously through twenty-five years of marriage and recalled how his wife once told him that if he agreed to stop drinking and give her the money instead, she'd be able to buy him a Cadillac at the end of a year! Looking back, Scott realizes that his wife may have been exaggerating, but he concedes that her point is valid: he's always spent a lot of money on expensive liquor.

When his wife died of cancer, their children were already grown, so Scott saw no reason to change his lifestyle. He continued drinking, no more (and no less) than ever. He acknowledged that, in relational terms, he'd had a *serious relationship* with alcohol through the first fifteen years of his marriage and that he probably had a *commitment* to it through the last ten. Scott also knew that his serious relationship, and later his commitment to drinking, had led to a good deal of resentment on the part of his wife, although she stayed with him out of a sense of commitment to marriage and their family.

After Scott's annual physical two years ago, his doctor told him that his liver was not functioning at 100 percent, and for the first time, he asked Scott about his drinking. Scott acknowledged drinking daily, but he minimized how much he actually drank. When his doctor recommended cutting down on his drinking, Scott did so, but only for a few weeks.

Around the same time, Scott had started dating Rachel, a woman he'd met at the local senior center where they both volunteered. They were good companions, he said, but he had no intention of marrying again: "One time on the marriage merry-go-round is enough for me!" he said with a laugh. But the counselor he'd seen on and off since his wife's death questioned whether this was the only reason Scott was keeping a distance in this relationship. For example, through questioning, the counselor learned that Scott had kept the extent of his drinking secret from Rachel. He would drink before they went out, for instance, in order to get "a head start." He would take her to restaurants that had bars, and usually at least once while they were eating, he'd excuse himself to use the restroom, only to stop for a "quick one" at the bar before returning to the table.

When asked about this behavior, Scott first blushed, then laughed. "Well," he said to the counselor, "I guess you could say I still have *two* women in my life—Rachel and my 'other girlfriend,' booze."

• • •

One could reasonably argue that Scott was not an *almost* alcoholic, but an alcoholic. It was clear that he had moved all the way through the zone that defines the almost alcoholic, to the point where his life now revolved around drinking. It was also likely that his blood alcohol level probably never reached zero, because his damaged liver was probably incapable of metabolizing all the ethanol he consumed. He was most likely on the way to a major health crisis. Finally, he had room in his life only for very limited human relationships, as his primary commitment was to alcohol.

Shannon's Story

Shannon's is a story of a serious relationship with drinking that developed over time but stopped short of the commitment that Scott had made. A nurse whose passion was working in the emergency department (ED) of a major urban hospital, Shannon was bright and energetic. Like many health care professionals who gravitate to ED work, she was intense yet able to act in a calm, deliberate fashion under stress that was often extreme.

Six years earlier Shannon had been diagnosed with stage II breast cancer. Fortunately, even though the cancer had spread to a second location in her breast, it had nevertheless been diagnosed fairly early. Still, Shannon's treatment had included chemotherapy, radiation therapy, and a partial mastectomy. It had been a grueling ordeal but she had survived and, although she would always be at some risk for a recurrence, she had recently passed the critical five-year threshold.

About a year after her treatment was completed, Shannon's

husband abruptly announced that he'd fallen in love with another woman and was leaving her and their four-year-old daughter. A couple of months later—and before the divorce was even final—Shannon was shocked again to learn that her husband's new girlfriend was pregnant.

Shannon had never been more than an occasional social drinker. After her separation, though, she began to drink more. Moreover, she began to drink alone. She justified having a glass of wine after work with the thought that it helped relieve the stress from working in an emergency department and being a single mother. This was true enough. It was also true that Shannon believed the glass of wine helped "take the edge off" and allow her to relax more around her daughter, now seven. Even at this stage, and even without any obvious negative consequences related to drinking, Shannon had progressed to the point where she had established a serious relationship with alcohol—she had crossed the border into the territory that defines the almost alcoholic. And although she was a nurse, Shannon was not aware that her daily drinking could increase her risk for a recurrence of cancer.

It was our opinion that at this early stage of the relationship, Shannon could have decided to turn back and return to normal social drinking. But she didn't.

Although Shannon continued to enjoy her evening wine, there were nights when she did not drink at all, for example, if she had to take her daughter to the art or karate classes that the girl enjoyed so much. On the other hand, when she did drink, Shannon's intake had gradually increased—from one to three or more glasses of wine. On some of these occasions, she would fall asleep on the family room couch after putting her daughter to bed. Once in a while she would wake the next morning feeling lethargic and groggy. At this point Shannon was even deeper into her serious relationship with alcohol. She had come to rely on her wine—it had become her buddy.

A turning point for Shannon came on one of those nights when she had put her daughter to bed and then gone into the family room for "one more glass of wine" while she caught the news before going to bed. She fell asleep and at some point had a dream about some kind of knocking sound. Then she awoke with a start, realizing the sound was no dream, but rather a loud banging coming from the rear of the house. And not only was there banging, but screaming as well, which Shannon instantly recognized as her daughter's voice.

Scrambling to her feet, Shannon ran to the back door. As she got closer, she saw her daughter's face through the window of the door. When their eyes met, the girl's eyes instantly filled with tears. Shannon threw open the door and they hugged.

Shannon eventually learned that after she had put her daughter to bed that night, the girl had fallen asleep briefly but then woke up thinking she'd forgotten to let their pet cat in for the night. When Shannon's daughter opened the back door to call for the cat, the door closed and locked behind her. First, she tried the door, and when it wouldn't open, she knocked. Then, when she got no response, she started to pound on the door. Finally, she pounded and called out, "Mommy!" Although it didn't actually take that long for Shannon to waken from her alcohol-induced sleep, realize what was happening, and rush to the door, it had seemed like an eternity to the girl.

Shannon's serious relationship with alcohol ended that night—and perhaps none too soon. She had already been developing some signs of moving further into the almost alcoholic gray area toward a commitment to drinking; she may even have moved into full dependency if she had drunk heavily enough long enough. With that in mind, and working collaboratively with one of the authors, she took several steps toward the goal of reversing course. First, she made (and kept) a commitment to abstain from drinking completely for at least six months. Significantly, she did not report having any cravings to drink. On the other hand, she and her counselor both recognized that she had established a habit of drinking at night; therefore, she would need to substitute a different (and healthier) habit. She chose exercise for this. She signed herself and her daughter up for membership at a community center where they went at least three times a week before dinner and swam, rode exercise bicycles, climbed walls, and so on.

In addition to these changes in routine, plus counseling, Shannon went online and found a cancer survivors support group for women who, like her, were health care professionals. Even though she'd been officially in remission for five years, she (like some other women she knew) still worried on some level about her health. "I go to the doctor a lot more often than I did before the diagnosis," she explained. "And every ache and pain seems to worry me. It's like I don't trust my body the way I once did." Shannon believed that this ongoing, underlying anxiety, along with her stressful job and unresolved feelings about her marriage, may all have contributed to her turning to alcohol as a way of coping. "I think that worked at first," she said, "but I can also see where it led me."

It was through her online support group that Shannon learned how drinking could increase her risk for a recurrence of cancer. This only increased her motivation to quit. "My daughter," she said, "is way more important than my cabernet."

Once in a while Shannon goes to a women's open AA meeting near her house. Such meetings are "open" in the sense that they welcome both true alcoholics and people who do not identify themselves as alcoholics. "I find it comforting somehow to listen to their stories," Shannon explained, "and realize that it could have happened to me. I've also made a couple of friends there."

What Is Your Relationship with Drinking?

You can use the following table and the descriptions of the three stages of drinking to help you determine what kind of relationship you (or someone you love) have with drinking.

The Drinking World

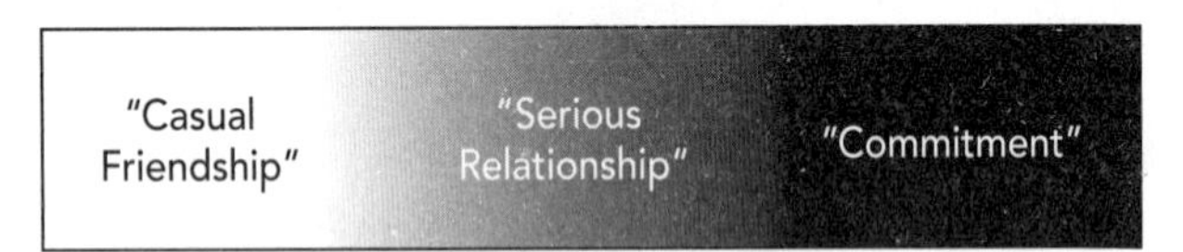

As before, there are no sharp lines marking the boundaries between the three kinds of relationships that a person who drinks can have with alcohol. Instead, they are separated by fairly large gray areas. These more accurately represent the process that people can pass through as their drinking changes over time. As we said at the outset, this process tends to be a gradual one. People do not wake up one morning to find that they are now suddenly alcoholics whereas yesterday they were normal social drinkers. Neither do they wake up one morning to discover that they now have a commitment to alcohol, when only the day before it was no more than a casual friendship.

You can use your journal and the following checklist as a guide to decide how far you or your loved one's relationship with alcohol has progressed.

"Casual Friendship"

___ Drinks almost always in social situations and seldom drinks alone

___ Rarely, if ever, has had a hangover

___ No significant personality changes when drinking versus not drinking

"Serious Relationship"

___ Drinks alone as often as or more often than in social situations

___ Drinks to feel good

___ Drinks to relieve stress or anxiety

___ Personality changes when drinking versus not drinking (more outgoing, less shy, more assertive, etc.)

___ Rarely ventures far from places where alcohol is available

___ Some significant others begin to feel jealous and resentful of the drinker's "relationship" with alcohol

___ May have some "unexplained" medical problems

___ Drinking begins to interfere with other roles, such as spouse, parent, or employee

QUIZ CONTINUED ON NEXT PAGE

"Commitment"

___ Drinks alone as well as *before* going to social occasions

___ Has had significant negative consequences clearly connected to drinking, such as

  ___ legal problems (DUI arrest, etc.)

  ___ relationship problems (conflict over drinking, aggression, etc.)

  ___ health problems

  ___ work problems

___ Becomes a "different person" when drinking and is irritable and unhappy when not drinking

___ Significant others deeply resent alcohol and are alienated from the drinker

___ Is not able to function adequately as a partner or parent

If you or someone you love is developing a serious relationship with alcohol but has not yet made a commitment to drinking, you can consider yourself (or your loved one) to be an almost alcoholic. There may still be time to make a course correction. (We'll be talking about strategies for doing that in part 2 of the book.) On the other hand, if drinking continues at its current pace (or increases), there is a good chance you could move on to the commitment stage. Once there, few if any drinkers can pull away from the commitment and return to even a serious relationship, much less the casual friendship characteristic of normal social drinkers—at least not without help.

4

Making the Decision to Change

Annette, in her early fifties, is married and has two children, a senior in high school and a junior in college. She had recently sought counseling for what she described as mild depression and, during an early counseling session, she disclosed that her husband has expressed concern about her drinking. Annette allows that she's always been someone who enjoyed a glass of wine, but rarely more than that. She usually drank in the company of her husband, in the evening, and she did not drink every night.

After her mother died following a year-long battle with lung cancer, Annette's drinking increased. She also started to drink alone, and now she drinks just about every day. She is frank in admitting that her mother's death was a blow. "It was especially hard seeing a strong woman slowly fall apart and die, bit by bit," she explained, relating how the chemotherapy seemed to sap all the strength from her mother. "I believe it would actually have been easier for me if she had died suddenly," Annette, who is an only child, explained.

According to Annette, she began to have trouble falling asleep at night about two months after her mother's death. She says that when she then started drinking some brandy before bed, she was able to get to sleep. However, within a few months it was taking two brandies to get to sleep. Even then, she often wakes up at two or three in the morning and has a hard time getting back to sleep. Meanwhile, her intake of wine in the evening had also increased to two or three glasses a night.

Annette does not believe she has a "drinking problem"; rather, she believes she has a "sleeping problem" and also may be "a little depressed." She says her husband has not suggested she has a drinking problem either, but has only pointed out the change in her drinking behavior and asked Annette if it wouldn't be a bad idea to cut down.

From our perspective, Annette probably had two very real "problems," the first being a lingering depression related at least in part to her mother's death. Second, she was now an almost alcoholic. The counselor suggested that Annette should indeed see if she could cut back on her drinking. He also suggested that she attend a few AA meetings and listen to the stories being told. He was pretty sure that Annette would be able to see herself in the early stages of some of those stories.

Annette did cut back on her drinking, but her effort was short lived. Scarcely a month later, her drinking was back at the same level it had been when her husband mentioned it. Meanwhile, she said that she did not identify in any way with the stories she'd heard at the AA meetings. Those men and women, she said, had "destroyed their lives," whereas she saw her own life as very much intact.

As Annette's counseling continued, her counselor delved further into changes in her personal life, including the death of her mother, and how these might correlate with her changed drinking pattern. It soon became apparent that, in addition to mourning her mother, Annette was mourning the impending loss of her youngest child, a daughter who would soon be leaving home to attend college. Her older son had done that three years earlier. Annette was now facing an "empty nest" in addition to missing her mother—little wonder she was "a little depressed"!

• • •

In the beginning, people who drink to medicate feelings don't usually consider the possibility that alcohol can cause problems; they drink because they believe it helps them. In Annette's case, for example, a brandy before bedtime initially helped her fall asleep. At first, Annette probably drank for the same reasons that most people drink: to enjoy the taste and, as an added "benefit," to make themselves feel better—more relaxed, less inhibited, or perhaps a little high or euphoric. Normal, social drinking works on that level—it's our "casual friend."

As Annette began to face some dramatic and stressful changes in her life, she entered the gray area of our drinking spectrum: she drank in an effort to make bad feelings—unexpressed grief that had turned into anxiety and depression—go away. After a couple of drinks, the relaxing effects of alcohol begin to give way to its depressant effects on the body and the mood. Even in relatively small amounts, alcohol slows our metabolism as well as our reflexes (which is what makes driving after drinking dangerous). Alcohol also has a disinhibiting effect on emotions. That's why people not only feel more relaxed after a few drinks, but also find themselves crying more easily or, alternatively, getting angry more easily.

Once the alcohol is metabolized by our bodies, the anxiety, self-consciousness, or whatever other emotion the alcohol had been temporarily masking will reemerge. That can lead us to move further along the drinking spectrum, as these uncomfortable feelings will reinforce the urge to drink again. This is where Annette was.

To compensate for her depression, Annette had developed a "serious relationship" with alcohol. Through drinking, she sought comfort for her depression, relief for her anxiety, and help in falling asleep. Initially alcohol did all those things for her. However, as her body developed a tolerance for alcohol, her "buddy" began to desert her. In fact, since Annette was drinking at the level where alcohol is very much a depressant, it was probably worsening, not helping, Annette's depression. Her drinking was also disrupting her sleep pattern, which can also contribute to depression. As long as Annette insisted on turning her friendship into a serious relationship—instead of substituting, for example, counseling plus medication—she was likely to move deeper into the almost alcoholic zone.

Drinking and Emotional Problems

Several common mental illnesses often accompany almost alcoholic behavior and may, as in Annette's case, even fuel it. It's pretty clear, for example, that the combination of mourning and the prospect of an empty nest made Annette depressed and that she drank in an effort to deal with that depression. In addition to anxiety disorders and depression, conditions that often promote drinking include attention deficit hyperactivity disorder (ADHD), eating disorders, bipolar disorder, and post-traumatic stress disorder (PTSD). Consider, for example, that the Epidemiologic Catchment Area Study of 20,000 people—one of the most comprehensive mental health surveys ever conducted in the United States—found that 13 percent of people with mental disorders also have alcohol problems.[14] Likewise, early work in the field of ADHD shows that the disorder often coexists with alcohol abuse. A study conducted at UCLA also found that approximately 50 percent of adults with ADHD are also substance abusers, 40 percent have anxiety disorders, 35 percent have major depression, 20 percent have learning disorders, and 10 percent have bipolar disorder.[15] Finally, soldiers who've served in Iraq or Afghanistan are at high risk for PTSD, and statistics show that they are also at risk for developing drinking problems.[16]

Research also shows that it's not just the number of symptoms a person has that is important; rather, it is the type of symptom. It is one story if an almost alcoholic has trouble sleeping and quite another if he or she has suicidal thoughts as a result of drinking. In the latter case, immediate intervention may be necessary to save a life. It is not possible to predict precisely at what point the effects of drinking will shift from interfering with sleep, as it did for Annette, to triggering self-destructive thoughts. Our point is that drinking that goes beyond the normal social level can be like playing with fire.

The Answer to "Why Do I Drink?" Can Change

As mentioned previously, people drink (or at least begin drinking) for one of two reasons:

- To create or enhance a *positive* feeling or a *desired* behavior
- To reduce or mask a *negative* feeling or *undesirable* behavior

Think about the days when you began to drink, in other words, when you were at the normal, social end of the drinking spectrum—when alcohol was no more than a casual friend. Use your journal to log your answers to the following questions:

What kind of *feeling* did you get when you drank? Did drinking make you feel

___ happy?

___ silly?

___ self-confident?

How did drinking affect your *behavior*? Did it help you to be

___ more outgoing?

___ more assertive?

___ more talkative?

Next, think about how drinking affects your behavior *now* in each of the above areas. Does it do for you today what it did for you in the beginning? For example, does it make you feel happier and outgoing, or does drinking now just make you sluggish and moody?

• • •

Next, consider whether, when you first started drinking, you may have been doing so, in part at least, to avoid or reduce negative feelings or behaviors, such as getting over social anxiety. One woman, Maggie, told us that she'd never drunk more than an occasional glass of wine with friends until, at age twenty-eight, she began to worry that she would never find a good relationship or realize her dream of being married and having children. It was at that point, she explained, that she began hanging out with a few single women she knew who liked to frequent sports bars in the hope of meeting single men.

"I discovered how a martini could break me out of my shell," Maggie said. "I'd always been painfully shy, which I believed was the main reason I did not seem to attract men. I thought they picked up on my shyness and felt awkward or else thought that I just didn't like them."

Drinking did, at least initially, produce this desirable effect for Maggie. She was an attractive woman, and that plus her martini-induced relaxed state opened the door to meeting men and dating. The problem was she quickly found that she had to drink not only to go out with friends but also before a date came to pick her up.

Soon Maggie had developed a habit of being mildly intoxicated whenever she was out on a date. Most of the time the men she dated drank as well, and they had a good time together. However, none of these dates ever developed into a relationship. Through counseling, Maggie eventually recognized that she had developed a "serious relationship" with alcohol.

Ask yourself the following questions and log your answers in your journal:

Was there a particular uncomfortable *emotion* that I tried to compensate for by drinking? For example, did I drink to overcome

____ anxiety?

____ depression?

____ anger or resentment?

____ jealousy?

Did I begin drinking in order to help overcome some *behavior* in myself that I was unhappy about? For example, did I drink because it helped me be less

____ shy?

____ socially awkward?

____ aggressive?

Now once again consider whether or not drinking *today* still helps you overcome any negative feelings or behaviors. Or has drinking lost some (or all) of its beneficial effects? Has drinking, as it did for Maggie, actually created new problems for you?

• • •

So far in this chapter we've examined the almost alcoholic and asked some questions to help you better understand why you drink. If you answered these questions honestly, you should have gained some insight into why you may have begun drinking—what drinking did for you—and whether you continue to reap those benefits from drinking versus experiencing other problems.

Are You Ready for a Change?

We have defined what it means to be almost alcoholic, how being an almost alcoholic differs from both normal social drinking and alcoholism, and what it means to have a "serious relationship" or "commitment" to drinking, as opposed to being a normal social drinker. If you are willing to keep an open mind and be honest with yourself, the material we've presented so far should help you determine where you (or a loved one) stands with respect to drinking. You may even have gained some insight, from the stories of others, about any factors that motivate your drinking.

In part 2 of this book, we will present strategies for changing, no matter where you (or your loved one) are on the drinking spectrum and what type of relationship you have with alcohol. Before we get to that, however, we think it's important to not assume that you *want* to change. We know that strategies for change are useful only for those individuals who are *ready for a change.*

The questionnaire that follows has been developed to help people determine just how ready they are for a change—from not at all to very much.[17] It's important to be as honest as possible when answering each question. Although we all want to present ourselves in a positive light, assessing your drinking and your readiness for change are not reflections on your character. There are, after all, millions of almost alcoholics. Drinking may be causing problems in their lives and insidiously impairing their health, but they do not make that connection. For the most part, they believe that they are keeping their lives together and being productive. They've crossed the line separating normal social drinking and moved into the grey area that defines almost alcoholic drinking, but not because they woke up one morning and decided that they wanted to do that or are weak willed. Rather, almost alcoholic drinking sneaked up on them. It is easy to do this, as literally millions of people, young and old, have found out.

Are you ready to learn just how ready you are for a change? If so, using the following scale respond to each of the statements in the Readiness for Change questionnaire and log your answers in your journal:

0 = I *disagree*
1 = I'm *undecided*
2 = I *agree*

When you are finished, total up your score.

• • •

Your score on the Readiness for Change questionnaire can range from 0 to 28. In our experience, few people have scores that lie at either extreme, though some do. In other words, few people are *totally not ready* for change, and equally few are *totally ready* for change. Most people with scores of 14 and over are fairly open-minded and, therefore, willing and able to benefit from the strategies in part 2 of this book.

Where do you fall—between totally ready and totally not ready—in terms of your readiness for change? Are you willing to at least consider changing your drinking behavior, or are you ruling that out altogether? Are you willing to keep an open mind and try some of the suggestions we will be presenting in part 2? What would you stand to lose if you did try a few of our ideas?

Readiness for Change Scale

	Disagree	Undecided	Agree
As far as I'm concerned, I have a problem that needs changing.	0	1	2
I think I might be ready for some self-improvement.	0	1	2
I am doing something about a problem that has been bothering me.	0	1	2
It worries me that I might slip back on a problem I have already changed, so I am looking for help.	0	1	2
I am finally doing some work on a problem I have.	0	1	2
I've been thinking that I might want to change something about myself.	0	1	2
At times my problem is difficult, but I am working on it.	0	1	2
I'd like to understand myself and my behavior better.	0	1	2
I have a problem and I really think I should work on it.	0	1	2
I have not been following through with something I've already changed and I want to prevent a relapse of the problem.	0	1	2
I thought I had once resolved this problem, but sometimes I find myself still struggling with it.	0	1	2
I'd like to hear some ideas on how to solve my problem.	0	1	2
Anyone can talk about changing, but I am actually doing something about it.	0	1	2
Even though I am not always successful at changing, at least I am trying.	0	1	2
Total score:			

Incidentally, although we are talking about drinking here, you can apply this questionnaire to *any* problem in your life. For now, visualize yourself as standing at the starting point of an adventure. Yes—an *adventure!* We think of this as an adventure, because whenever we make a decision to change established habits, we are essentially stepping into uncharted territory. Believe us, it's impossible to know just how much your life as a whole can change for the better if you decide to pursue some of the changes we will suggest. Many people have told us that they were surprised by how one change can lead to others, leading to a snowball effect that ends in a profoundly different—and more satisfying—lifestyle.

Feel free to rethink any or all of the provided questions at any time and to reconsider your readiness for change.

Part 2

Solutions for the Almost Alcoholic

5

Looking at the Man (or Woman) in the Mirror

Jacob, a thirty-five-year-old college professor, decided to "take a break from drinking" after two separate work-related events occurred: he got the worst student evaluations in his four years of teaching and two of his papers were turned down by journals that had previously accepted his work. For Jacob, these experiences amounted to a wake-up call. He knew that he would be facing his department's tenure committee the coming year, and neither of these things would help his cause.

Divorced for a little over a year and with no children, Jacob had settled into a fairly isolated lifestyle. He was punctual for his classes, kept regular office hours, and attended all faculty meetings—but other than that, he interacted little with others. Although he did regularly attend the college's basketball games, he spent most of his free time in his small home, located about half an hour from campus.

In that past year Jacob had increased his drinking significantly. He didn't realize it might be affecting him, though, until the rejections and the student reviews came in. That was when he decided to take a break.

Thus far, Jacob's life had been what he himself described as "a smooth road." One of three children of a successful professional couple, he'd excelled in school as well as sports. He graduated college near the top of his class and then went on to graduate school, where he did equally well. It was in grad school that he'd met his wife, Dana. They had been married for four years when she started talking about being unhappy. A trained social worker, she found her work with a social agency charged with child protection to be both stressful and frustrating. When she told Jacob that she'd been thinking about trying to get pregnant and taking some time off, he hesitated, saying that he'd prefer to wait until after he got tenure. Then she abruptly declared that she didn't think she wanted a child after all.

A year later, Dana suddenly announced that she'd fallen in love with another man and wanted a divorce. Jacob was not entirely surprised—even though they had avoided talking about it, Dana's unhappiness had been evident to him. As divorces go, it was amicable. Eight months later, Jacob learned through a mutual friend that Dana was pregnant.

Although Jacob's life may have been a "smooth road" up until his marriage ended, he had not found his position as an assistant professor all that rewarding for some time. It was ironic, he explained to a counselor he'd sought out, because securing a college teaching position had been his goal for as long as he could remember. "I know plenty of people," he said, "who would give their eye teeth to be in my position. New assistant professorships are incredibly competitive."

His good fortune notwithstanding, Jacob found that he was progressively losing interest in teaching. That, plus his divorce and the resulting social isolation, no doubt had contributed to his moving into the almost alcoholic zone. As he described it, "On one level, I do like teaching. Most of my students are motivated, and a few are truly bright. Yet my life has come to feel kind of sterile—giving lectures, grading papers, giving tests."

Jacob's one close friend was the college's basketball coach, a man twenty years Jacob's elder. The two men had connected over basketball—Jacob had played the game through high school and college. Jacob and coach Tim would meet for lunch in the faculty club's dining hall every couple of months, and it was during their last lunch that Jacob, on impulse, had told his friend about the student ratings and the journal rejections. Tim then invited Jacob to join him and his wife for a barbecue the following weekend—just the three of them.

While Tim's wife busied herself with a huge salad and Tim cooked steaks, Jacob declined Tim's offer of a beer. "To tell the truth, I've been drinking more since the divorce," he said, "and I think that it may have been affecting me. I haven't had a drink now in about a month."

Tim's reply was quick: "Good for you, Jake. Take a good long break from it. It will let your head clear. To me, it sounds like it's gotten pretty foggy in there." Jacob laughed and nodded in agreement.

In the course of a leisurely after-dinner conversation, Jacob asked Tim if he'd ever felt bored or unfulfilled with his work and, if so, what he had done about it. Tim replied, "Not exactly bored, but in a way, unfulfilled. My teams have a long track record of success. That's great. But at the same time, I've always been a superstitious man. In fact, the more successful my teams were, the more superstitious I was that something bad would happen. It all seemed too—"

"Smooth?" Jacob interjected. Tim nodded. "Yeah, too smooth," he said, "like life shouldn't be such a smooth road."

Jacob explained that he felt that way as well, but didn't know what to do about it. Then Tim spoke up: "I can tell you what I did about it, and what all the boys on my team are required to do about the fact that they are so naturally gifted and blessed."

Jacob listened intently as Tim explained how, many years earlier in his career, he had been plagued by this feeling that things were going too well for him—that he was doing "a lot of getting but not much giving." The solution came to him when he met the director of a local camp for disabled children at a fund-raiser. In an instant, Tim said, he knew that he wanted to become part of that organization. His offer was quickly accepted, and Tim went on to become not only an occasional volunteer coach, but also a spokesperson for the camp, which relied heavily on charitable contributions. He even chaired the committee that raised money for a new gymnasium featuring equipment accessible to the disabled.

Listening to Tim, Jacob felt that a light went off in his head as well. In his next counseling session, he told his therapist that while he did not yet have a solution, he now understood what the problem was. "I really don't dislike teaching," he explained, "but I know now that it is not enough. I need to find more meaning in life than that." And he'd begun to explore ways of doing that, beginning by joining the local Lions Club and participating in its charitable activities. "Last Sunday, I flipped pancakes on the town green to raise money for children's books for the library," he told his therapist. "I had a great time."

• • •

Moments of insight like both Tim and Jacob had are what most people consider *epiphanies:* new ways of seeing ourselves in relation to the world around us. They can be truly life changing. In the many stories we have heard from almost alcoholics who were able to either stop altogether or return to normal social drinking, two factors seemed to facilitate experiences like the one Jacob had:

- *Not drinking.* Simply put, men and women who have been living in the almost alcoholic zone for a long time lose sight of just how much drinking has affected the way they see the world and their place in it. Several almost alcoholics describe their former perspective as "seeing the world through partially frosted glass." This is especially true for those almost alcoholics whose drinking behavior includes "maintaining a buzz," for example, by sipping drinks over a prolonged period of time. By doing so, they maintain a blood alcohol level that is undoubtedly higher than the legal limit but somewhat lower than it would be if they drank more quickly. These almost alcoholics like the way this kind of drinking feels, and they are usually unaware of how it is harming their health. Similarly, they usually don't realize how the alcohol is deadening their senses and slowing their thinking. If these almost alcoholics decide to stop drinking for a while—say, a few months—they are often surprised at how much more alert and perceptive they are. As one woman put it, "It was like I was seeing life through a pair of sunglasses, and then the lenses gradually cleared."

- *Being open to self-examination.* Almost alcoholic drinking not only dulls the senses but also sedates the drinker. This state of mind is not conducive to reflection. In fact, as we stated earlier, many almost alcoholics drink to avoid certain emotions or thoughts: "I drink so I don't have to think," said one man who had lost his wife to cancer and subsequently entered the almost alcoholic zone. Although his decision to drink and thereby anesthetize his grief may have made sense to this man, it also diminished his life to a significant degree. When they decide to try not drinking for a while, many almost alcoholics discover that their eyes are suddenly open and that they are able to confront issues they may have avoided for years by drinking.

If you have decided that you are ready to change the way you drink, you may also discover that doing so allows you to see the world through a different set of "lenses." Your thinking may become a bit clearer, your emotions may become less dull and more accessible to you, and you are able to reflect on issues that you've avoided for a long time.

When people say that they've had an *epiphany*, what they usually mean is that they are able to see themselves from a new perspective. For some people, this happens suddenly—a sort of "Aha!" experience—but for others, the process of self-evaluation occurs more slowly over a period of time. In either case, this new perspective on themselves is often accompanied by a shift of some sort—in the way they think of themselves, their goals, or their sense of purpose. A famous and quite dramatic example is Bill Wilson, cofounder of Alcoholics Anonymous (AA), who wrote about an epiphany he had while lying in a hospital bed, close to death from his drinking. It was then that he experienced a clear sense of being released from the grip of alcohol by a power greater than himself. That vision, he claimed, motivated him to turn to others for help in staying sober, as opposed to trying to do that through sheer willpower, as he'd been doing until then.

Although their experiences are usually less dramatic, it's surprising just how many people say that, at some point in their lives, they'd also had an epiphany that had a positive effect on their lives. This was true for both Tim and Jacob. Their experiences were strong enough to clarify their goals and values, change their opinion of themselves, and alter their lifestyles.

It is most significant that people repeatedly tell us these experiences have occurred when they were sober. As Tim told Jacob, not drinking would allow the "fog" in his head to clear. It is as though drinking acted as a veil between Jacob and the possibility of epiphany and change.

Who Are You? Taking a Personal Inventory

There are some typical ways in which we define who we are. These include our marital status (married, divorced, or single), whether we are parents, and what we do for a living. Often these descriptors help to define, at least in part, our lifestyles. For example, we know that a man who is in his thirties or forties, works as an accountant, and is married with two children is apt to be a pretty busy person with a middle-class lifestyle. But that doesn't tell us very much about what that same man *thinks* of himself or how he *feels* about his lifestyle. It doesn't tell us much about his goals, values, or priorities. It doesn't reveal anything about what he believes his purpose in life might be or whether he is satisfied with himself.

Being an almost alcoholic is actually one piece of a person's identity, just as one's occupation is a piece of his or her identity, because it also tells us something about the person's lifestyle. Being an almost alcoholic, however, does not say anything about a person's character, any more than his or her occupation does. What we do know is that as long as people remain in the almost alcoholic zone, their thinking will remain more or less clouded, and they will be unlikely to be open to insight—much less an epiphany—that could change their lives for the better.

Part of the solution for the almost alcoholic, then, can include looking inward and taking a fresh look at who you are and who you'd like to be. We will be discussing many more specific solutions in the chapters that follow, but if you're willing, let's step back and do a bit of reflecting right now. This exercise will be more helpful if you are willing and able to take a break from drinking for a set amount of time, such as a month. This will allow your head to clear—at least enough so that you can be open to a new perspective and new thoughts about yourself, where your life is, and where you might like it to go. Is simply deciding to look inward and examine your life a surefire way to have an epiphany? Probably not. On the other hand, it is possible to begin a process of self-reflection that has the potential to be life changing. To begin, take a few moments to reflect on who you are right now. Think about your occupation and how you feel about it, your personal life and how you feel about it, and your drinking behavior that places you somewhere in the almost alcoholic zone—just how far from normal social drinking you are, only you can tell.

Your identity does not end with your occupation, your role in your family, and your lifestyle. It runs deeper than that. If you have read this far, chances are you've decided that you are ready for a change. If so, get out your journal and take some time to reflect on not one but a pair of questions. This is a proven teaching and learning technique called *dialectics.*[18] Presenting questions in pairs helps you engage in an inner dialogue that pits one question against the other. This technique promotes insight—and can even trigger an epiphany!

"Who Am I?" versus "Who Have I Thought I Should Be?"

Many men and women who long ago gave up drinking attest to how dramatically different their lives are now compared to when they were alcoholics or almost alcoholics. They say that they'd spent years trying to be someone, live a certain lifestyle, or pursue goals that they did not feel any real passion for, but as long as they could use alcohol to mask their inner unhappiness, they went through life in an almost robotic manner.

"For years I'd just wake up every morning, put one foot in front of the other, and get through the day," said Jeff, who in his early twenties had given in to pressures to join his family's construction business rather than pursuing his interest in literature and teaching. So he'd earned a bachelor's degree in management (instead of English) and become a manager (instead of a teacher).

Viewed from the outside, Jeff's life looked fine. He earned a decent income, had a nice house, was married with three children, and could afford to take the family on a nice vacation every year. On the inside, though, things were different. Jeff, now forty-three, had been an almost alcoholic for nearly fifteen years. He drank every day—not enough to get drunk or pass out, but enough to stay high and fall asleep early. His wife and children had long grown used to this pattern and didn't question Jeff's drinking.

Jeff was always kind, never mean, went to work every day, and was a good provider. The problem was Jeff felt unfulfilled. He loved his wife and children, and he was grateful that they were able to live a good lifestyle. Still, he drank to compensate for a deep and lingering feeling of unhappiness. On occasion, his wife Terry, who sensed her husband's discontent, would gently confront him about it, asking something like, "Why are you unhappy, Jeff? We have a good life. Are you unhappy with me or the kids?" Jeff would reply to these inquiries with assurances that he was, indeed, happy. He'd then brush it off by saying that he was "prone to depression." The conversation never went deeper than that.

Two events led Jeff to change his drinking behavior. The first was physical: his doctor diagnosed him with type 2 diabetes, as well as borderline hypertension. The doctor asked Jeff about his drinking. Jeff minimized it, but the doctor still advised him to stop. "Don't drink for a month," he said to Jeff, "and then let's rerun some tests."

Jeff did not like the doctor's advice. "The idea of not drinking for a week bothered me, not to mention a month!" he said. Then the second event happened. It was nothing dramatic—at least it wouldn't strike most people that way. His oldest child, a twelve-year-old daughter, won a story-writing competition at school. On the drive home after receiving her award certificate, the girl casually announced to her parents that she wanted to become a teacher someday. "I'd like to teach kids how to read and write stories," she said.

This comment lingered in Jeff's mind. At the time he'd not had a drink for five weeks—the longest he'd gone without at least one drink a day in more than twenty years. He said that it was still hard to resist his well-established habit of pouring himself a drink upon returning home from the office. To avoid that urge, as well as improve his overall health, Jeff had started stopping at the gym on his way home to swim or use a treadmill for half an hour. He found that this made it a bit easier to resist that urge to drink. He'd told Terry about his diagnoses as well as the doctor's advice, and she was completely supportive of this change in Jeff's daily routine.

Although he missed drinking, Jeff had to admit that after five weeks of abstinence, plus three weeks of regular exercise, he felt physically better than he had in a time. He had more energy during the day, was able to stay up until his wife went to bed, and woke up feeling more refreshed.

Jeff continued to mull over his daughter's comment. Then one day after work, he fired up the family computer—something he rarely did—and did some research on the web. A few days later a package arrived in the mail. The return address was "Literacy Volunteers." Jeff opened it so eagerly that Terry laughed. "You look like a kid opening a birthday present!" she said.

In a way, that package from the nonprofit Literacy Volunteers was indeed like a birthday present for Jeff, and he read it through voraciously. Two days later, after thinking about it and making a few calls, Jeff told Terry that he'd decided to sign up for training to become a literacy volunteer in their town. He would be sure that this activity did not take away too much time from the family, he said. On the other hand, he really wanted to do this. Terry replied that he shouldn't be concerned about taking the time. She'd never seen Jeff so excited about something, she said, and again she was totally supportive.

Jeff's story may not seem terribly dramatic. His decision to become a literacy volunteer may not strike you as an epiphany on the scale of Bill Wilson's. But an epiphany it was, and it changed Jeff's life by adding some much-needed balance and by providing him with a way to pursue his old interest in English and in the teaching career he'd never pursued. Equally important, this epiphany probably would never have happened as long as Jeff remained in the almost alcoholic zone.

Whose Life Are You Living?

After Jeff completed his training and was working about four hours a week as a literacy volunteer, he happened to mention it to his family at a Fourth of July barbecue. By that time, Jeff had not had a drink for several months. Although he did not consider himself an alcoholic, he was not sure that he would go back to drinking again, for two reasons. First, he really was feeling a lot better physically. He had a lot more energy and was enjoying his modified lifestyle, including exercise and his volunteer work. His doctor was confident that his diabetes could now be controlled without medication, but cautioned that this might not be the case if Jeff went back to drinking as he had before. That raised Jeff's second reservation: he was not sure that it was worth the risk to his health to even try to return to normal social drinking.

At the family barbecue, one of Jeff's brothers noticed that Jeff was drinking only iced tea and commented on it. Jeff just smiled and replied that his diabetes was under control without alcohol and he wanted to keep it that way. Then Jeff's father brought up his volunteer work in a teasing way. "Why would you want to spend your time teaching a bunch of illiterates to read?" he asked. "You're not even getting paid for it." Again, Jeff just smiled and said, "I like doing it. And sometimes the most meaningful things you can do are things you don't get paid for."

Later that day, after all the company had left, Terry brought up her father-in-law's comment and said she hadn't appreciated its teasing tone. Jeff replied that although that brief interaction may have seemed like a small matter, it had really been very meaningful for him. He explained that, in many ways, he had been "leading the life my father chose for me, and not one I might have chosen for myself." He did not blame his father for that, he said, as he knew that his father wanted only the best for his children, and that he'd pressed Jeff to pursue an education in business because he believed it would lead to success and financial security. "He was right about that," said Jeff. "But somewhere along the way, I forgot to balance my father's wishes with my own interests. I'm not really unhappy being a businessman, but it isn't enough. In a way I think I used alcohol for a long time to avoid thinking about that. I didn't expect my father to praise me for doing volunteer work, and I really don't need his approval for that."

A New You?

Alcoholics Anonymous is a peer recovery program for alcoholics. Almost alcoholic readers may or may not choose to attend open AA meetings and listen to the stories of addiction and recovery that are shared there. One thing that has struck us from speaking with many people and hearing their stories is just how dramatically their lives have improved after they stopped drinking. Whether an alcoholic or an almost alcoholic, becoming open to insights—or epiphanies—seems to be possible only when we have a clear head; Jeff's experience in the previous example demonstrated this.

Many almost alcoholics are not aware that they drink to smother feelings or avoid thinking about certain things. When they decide to stop drinking, even for a short period of time, they often experience emotions or reflect on questions that they've long avoided. This can be uncomfortable for a time—after all, it was those uncomfortable feelings that they were medicating with alcohol. But, as it did for Jeff, this can mark the starting point for a more fulfilling life.

Don't be surprised if changing your drinking behavior also marks the beginning of a deeper process of change—in fact, expect it. That's not to say you will turn your life upside down. On the other hand, such a change can lead to a new you in unique and significant ways. For Jeff, change was not necessarily dramatic. He did not quit his job or leave his family so he could write the "great American novel." Yet the changes he made were significant *for him* and led him to become a healthier man—physically, emotionally, and mentally.

The Man (or Woman) in the Mirror

One of the late Michael Jackson's hit songs bears the title "Man in the Mirror," and it is a song about self-reflection and taking charge of one's life. The story of Jeff is relevant to that song, and it may also be meaningful for you, especially with a clear, sober mind. Take a few minutes to reflect on the following pairs of questions. If you'd like, use your journal to sum up your thoughts. They may just mark the beginning of a change process for you.

"Who Am I?" versus "Who Should I Be?"

This was the essence of Jeff's dilemma because, to paraphrase his words, he'd spent a long time living his father's dream for him rather than his own. He began to strike a balance and live more of his own life when he was able to get in touch with some of his own core interests and values and then found a way to incorporate these into an expanded and more fulfilling life.

"What Do I Want?" versus "Why Am I Here?"

These questions ask you to compare and contrast any material desires you have with what you might call your emotional or spiritual needs. It is certainly true that we live in a material world. We are literally bombarded with skillful marketing techniques designed to create "needs": for a bigger home, a nicer car, grander vacations, and so on. Yet wise people know that material possessions alone do not make a lifestyle satisfying. Even billionaires like Bill Gates and famous and wealthy entertainers like Angelina Jolie have learned that life is richer and more satisfying when it has meaning to us beyond material success.

Ask yourself the following questions and jot down your answers in your journal:

- Do I have a purpose in life? What is that purpose?
- After I am gone, what would I like those closest to me to think and say about me?
- What, besides material possessions, would I want to bequeath to my loved ones?

"Where Have I Been?" versus "Where Am I Going?"

There is an old saying that goes something like this: "It isn't where you've been that matters; it's where you are going." The core message here is that the future is more important than the past and that we should go through life with our eyes looking forward, not backward.

Living is the past has its hazards, not the least of which is that it can lead us to a life filled with regrets. Jeff, for example, could have done that, feeling regretful that he had not pursued his original interests. But that would have gotten him nowhere. Worse still, it could have motivated him to drink even more in an effort to avoid those feelings. Instead, Jeff was able to pause, take a sober look at "the man in the mirror," and make some decisions about moving forward.

Asking yourself questions like the following and reflecting on them in your journal can be helpful in guiding you toward moving forward in your own life:

- What in my life gives me the most satisfaction? Is it my work? Family life? Community involvement? Hobbies?
- If someone asked me the question "What would you like to learn to do?" what would my answer be?
- What, if anything, have I "left behind" that might be worth a second look?

This chapter has explored what can happen if and when a person decides to move out of the alcoholic zone and takes some time to reflect. Whether the person occupies a space in that zone closer to normal social drinking or has moved further toward alcoholism, a mind that is not influenced by alcohol is the best mind for this undertaking. It is the first of many possible solutions we will be discussing for finding a way out of an almost alcoholic life.

6

Building a Support System

Considerable research has been conducted and reported on ways of helping people either stop drinking or return to normal social drinking. Many of those techniques will be shared here to supplement the self-assessment you just completed.

Social Support: A Two-Way Street

The largest study ever conducted on treatment for men and women with problems of either alcohol dependence or alcohol abuse included nearly 2,000 individuals recruited from nine treatment sites located throughout the United States.[19] The researchers followed this large group for ten years to see how well the different treatments worked and to identify the best predictors of success. One very significant finding from that research concerned the subjects' social support networks.

"People like people like themselves," goes an old saying. In other words, people tend to gravitate toward others whose behavior, attitudes, and even interests mirror their own. In many situations, that is not a problem. For example, most people who attend college basketball games or concerts do so precisely because they root for the same team or like the same bands or singers. There is nothing wrong with that.

When it comes to drinking, however, and specifically to trying to change your drinking behavior, this tendency toward affinity can indeed be a problem. In the long-term study just mentioned, one of the most powerful predictors of long-term success was what the researchers called "network support for drinking"—in other words, who the subjects in these studies spent most of their time with.[20] To cut to the chase: the more they surrounded themselves with people who drank a lot (and who saw nothing wrong with that), the more likely they were to return to drinking as much or more than they did before they reached out for help. This is significant because these were men and women who had already decided that they needed to do something about their drinking and went so far as to sign up for treatment. Here is an example.

Justin's Story

A licensed realtor, Justin had prospered for twenty years in the middle-class suburban town where he had been born and raised. Although the real estate boom that caught fire in many places in the country had not been so dramatic in his area, it had been strong enough to provide him with a steady stream of homes to be bought and sold. He was well known in the community and had a reputation—in a profession not always known for it—for being honest and working hard to help people find the right homes for their families and their budgets. Many of Justin's clients were men and women he'd known since childhood, and much of his business came to him by word of mouth.

As a high school senior, Justin had gone through a period of heavy drinking, as had several of his best friends. By the time they'd hit their late twenties, though, most (including Justin) had settled into a pattern of what might be called "ritualized social drinking." For example, Justin was accustomed to meeting several male friends on alternate Thursday nights after work for wings and beers at a local sports bar. And once a month he and his wife, Amanda, would gather with a group of friends for a Saturday night potluck get-together that rotated from home to home. Finally, on most nights Justin would enjoy a beer right after work while helping Amanda make dinner or checking in with their two children.

As happy as Amanda was with her and Justin's lifestyle, she had over the years expressed concern about two of his friends and their influence on her husband. Specifically, Amanda observed that on those occasions when Justin had gone to do something with these two men—and only these two men—there was a good chance he would come home noticeably under the influence. This had happened several times, for example when he'd gone with these friends to watch a minor league baseball game or a college football game at the sports bar. Each time Amanda explained her concern: Justin's career in the community rested in part on his reputation; arrests for driving while intoxicated were routinely printed in the local paper and posted online. If Justin's name ever appeared in either or both of these forums, it would surely hurt him and, by extension, their family.

Justin would listen to his wife on these occasions and then make a vague promise to drink less the next time he went out with these particular friends. What he didn't tell Amanda was that he'd already been stopped by the police once after one of these nights out for rolling through a stop sign. Fortunately for Justin, the officer recognized him, not only as a former classmate but as someone he ran into often at their kids' sporting events. He'd looked at Justin seriously and said, "I'm going to cut you a break today, my friend. I'm giving you a ticket for failing to stop at that stop sign back there. But what I'm not going to do is ask you to take a sobriety test."

As the officer turned to leave, he said over his shoulder, "Be careful the rest of the way home, Justin. There's another officer on patrol out there." Chastened by this close call, Justin did cut back on his nights out with these two buddies.

• • •

Again, we come back to a question often asked here: was Justin, at that point, an alcoholic? Based on the above information, the answer is probably not. On the other hand, was his drinking a problem? Yes, it was a problem.

By virtue of his occasional outings with his heavy-drinking buddies, Justin had already crossed the line into the almost alcoholic zone by the time he was pulled over by the police officer that night. He may not have been very far into that zone at that point, but two years later he was.

What happened in those two years was what came to be called "the great recession" in the United States and elsewhere in the world. It was a prolonged period marked by major financial collapse, lost wealth, and chronic high unemployment.

In large part it was led by a collapse in the worldwide housing and real estate markets—and Justin and his career got caught up in it.

At first, Justin responded to the economic hard times in the same way that many of his peers did—he worked harder. Never lazy to begin with, Justin made sure he was now available at all times to his clients. As it turned out, the vast majority of these were people who were trying to sell their homes. Prospective buyers, in contrast, were scarce. As a result, the buyers could afford to be extremely picky and often put in bids so low that the seller couldn't afford to sell. Not a few of his sellers had homes whose assessed value was considerably less than what was still owed on the mortgage—so-called underwater homes.

Of course, no amount of effort on Justin's part could reverse a global economic trend. Try as he might to make it otherwise, Justin's income plummeted. To help make up for it, Amanda signed on as a substitute teacher in their town. As that was not enough to close the gap, the family cut its expenses and trimmed luxury items as much as possible, such as vacations, going to the movies, and eating out.

Justin began spending longer hours at the office, editing his real estate listings to make them look as attractive as possible, sending out e-mails to any prospective buyers he could think of, and so on. At the same time, he drifted more toward the two men who'd been his drinking buddies before, while spending less time with friends who either didn't drink or drank very moderately. Although he did his best to hide it, in time Amanda noticed that Justin smelled of beer and was noticeably lethargic when he got home one or two nights a week. Then he had his second problem while driving, smashing the driver's side rearview mirror while pulling into the garage. That led to a confrontation with Amanda.

Whereas the effect of being pulled over by the police had frightened Justin and motivated him—at least for a time—to return to normal social drinking, the failing economy and the financial stress it was placing on his family was a force that pushed him back, and deeper, into the almost alcoholic zone. Of course, part of what motivated Justin to drink more was the stress he was under, and perhaps a bit of depression. However, that stress was not about to go away any time soon, so Justin needed to find another solution.

Consistent with what research has found, Justin's drift back into the almost alcoholic zone was accompanied by a parallel drift toward friends who drank more. Meanwhile, he spent less time with the nondrinking or social-drinking friends he and Amanda once hung out with regularly. And as research has also shown, the longer Justin chose to remain within the social network that supported almost alcoholic drinking, the harder it would be for him to escape.

Taking Stock of Your Social Network

If you have decided that you would like to change directions and move away from almost alcoholic drinking and toward normal social drinking—or no drinking at all—one helpful part of the solution will be to step back and honestly assess your social support network. You can begin by using your journal to record your answers to these questions:

1. For about how long, would you estimate, have you been drinking in an almost alcoholic way?

2. Think back to a time *before* you believe you crossed over into the almost alcoholic zone. Picture your life then.

3. Now, write down the names of the friends you socialized with most at that time.

4. Next, write down the names of any friends you were close to before you became an almost alcoholic but who have since dropped out of your social network.

5. Do you currently socialize with any men and women who are nondrinkers? If so, make three columns and write down their names, as well as how often you see these people and under what circumstances, using these headings: Name, How Often, and Where.

6. Write down the names of those friends you currently see most often. Among this group, using the criteria and examples presented so far in this book, can you identify one or more who you think might have a problem with alcohol? If so, make a list of those people.

7. Can you imagine yourself socializing with a group of friends and *not* drinking while you are in their company? If so, name some of the activities can you picture being involved in with them.

Although people have told us that they believe they could continue to hang out and otherwise socialize with friends who regularly drink—including some who could be almost alcoholics—without difficulty, research strongly suggests otherwise. Stories we've heard from men and women who'd tried this approach also suggest otherwise. Despite the best of intentions, it seems that our behavior does depend in part on who is with us. For some people this may include family members as well as friends, which can present a further complication.

In some communities, such as Amish enclaves, which are tightly knit social networks, alcohol abuse and alcoholism appear to be relatively rare. A likely explanation is that these communities represent social networks that support sobriety or social drinking, not excessive drinking in any form. Of course, few people live in such communities, although the principle remains the same: the more successfully you build a community of family and friends who do not support excessive drinking, the more successful your efforts to change are likely to be.

The Limits of Willpower

Greg's drinking was only one of his problems—he also had a problem with gambling. Naturally, the places he liked to hang out the most were casinos, and the people he liked to hang out with the most were people who also enjoyed gambling and drinking. Although neither drinking nor gambling had led him to ruin at this point, Greg had nevertheless suffered some significant financial losses at blackjack tables. Moreover, when he drank he gambled—100 percent of the time.

Despite this reality, Greg continued to believe (and tell his wife Margie, his minister, and eventually a counselor) that he believed he could stay sober and not gamble but still spend time with his friends at his favorite casino. His rationale was that he liked the "ambience" of a casino as well as its restaurants. "There's just so much energy in a casino!" he'd say. "I just love being there. I think I can enjoy it without gambling."

So far, this approach had failed not once, but three times. After the third failure—when Greg went to the casino, met up with his friends, drank, and lost $500—Margie put her foot down and insisted they talk to their minister. That meeting led to a referral to a counselor.

As we pointed out in the beginning of the book, when almost alcoholics do seek counseling, their drinking is often the last thing on their minds. When Greg went with Margie to see the counselor, he said he thought he was there for marriage counseling, not because of his drinking and gambling!

Testing the Bootstraps Theory

Our society has long valued personal willpower. We teach our children the virtues of independence, ambition, competitiveness, and drive. To some extent, we balance these values with an emphasis on teamwork. Still, the idea that we can "pull ourselves up by our bootstraps" has fairly deep roots in our collective consciousness. That is not necessarily a bad thing. Our history, for example, is filled with stories of people who succeeded, despite great odds, through perseverance and individual determination. Yet anyone who has played a team sport, run a successful business, or raised children also knows that success is not ultimately a matter of individual willpower alone. Hillary Clinton's book *It Takes a Village* speaks to how it takes an entire community to raise psychologically and spiritually healthy children.[21]

Similarly, the solution for being almost alcoholic needs to go beyond individual willpower. Both Greg and Justin, for example, had the best of intentions to control their drinking, yet those intentions alone proved insufficient. That brings us to the issue of your social network: how it affects you and how you may need to change it. First, though, we suggest taking out your journal and answering the following questions:

1. Have you ever been confronted with a problem that you could not solve all by yourself? What was that problem?
2. Have you ever set a goal that you could not achieve without help? What was that goal?
3. Name some people you have turned to in the past for help in overcoming a problem, achieving a goal, or both.
4. On a scale of 1 to 10, with 10 meaning *most willing,* how willing are you right now to accept the idea that willpower alone is not always enough to solve a problem or achieve a goal?
5. On the same scale of 1 to 10, with 10 meaning *most willing,* how willing are you to include some changes in your social network as part of your overall solution?

Justin's and Greg's Solutions

Let's get back to Justin and Greg and look at what they did to help themselves move out of the almost alcoholic zone. Part of their solution involved a shift in their social networks—*away* from a social network that supported almost alcoholic drinking and *toward* one that did not. That did not mean they needed to tell their friends that they were trying to change their drinking behavior, and neither Justin nor Greg chose to do so. Rather, it was through the simple act of shifting their social network that both Justin and Greg were in effect "reaching out" for help.

For Justin, the change involved telling his drinking buddies that his family's tightening budget meant giving up his nights of meeting for beers and wings. He did not say how long he would have to do this, nor did he say that he was doing this in order to change his drinking behavior. He was, on the other hand, quite firm in making this announcement.

This change proved to be significant, for by avoiding these social situations that heavily supported drinking, Justin was bolstering his personal determination to change. He stopped trying to pretend that he could spend time in a sports bar with friends who liked to drink but limit himself to drinking soda—or even one beer. "I know I like tap beer too much for that!" he said with a laugh. And because the reason he gave for making this change (and thereby shifting his social network) was financial, no one challenged him or tried to persuade him otherwise.

Rather than completely "abandoning" his old drinking buddies, Justin and Amanda decided to host monthly get-togethers at their home for their friends. Justin's drinking buddies (and their wives) would be invited, as would their friends who either did not drink or who drank very little. Alcoholic beverages would be limited (again, citing tight finances) and when these were gone, there would be no more. Finally, each couple would be asked to bring appetizers (but not alcohol) to share to keep the cost of these gatherings reasonable.

As it turned out, almost all of the couples that Justin and Amanda knew were also feeling the effects of a prolonged recession, and they appreciated the opportunity to socialize once a month without having to spend a lot of money. Justin's drinking buddies and their wives came to some of the get-togethers. If they did bring beer with them of their own accord, it was no more than a six-pack, which ended up being shared. Justin found that he had little difficulty substituting soda in those situations. Meanwhile, there were several couples who did not bring either wine or beer, saying that they preferred not to drink since they had to drive home.

Greg's solution had to begin with an acknowledgment that he and Margie were referred to a counselor not for marriage counseling, but due to the problems that his drinking and gambling were causing. He resisted that idea at first, but at the second counseling session, Margie presented Greg with a list of his net gambling losses over the past three years—$3,500—along with credit card records showing what Greg had spent on liquor and food each time he visited the casino.

Confronted with these stark realities, Greg finally accepted that he had a problem with drinking and that drinking pretty much always led to gambling (and vice versa). He did try to minimize his losses, saying he knew people who'd lost much more, but he did not try to deny that he liked to drink and gamble, that he lost money at the casino, and that his losses had grown bigger each year.

Greg's solution, like Justin's, involved a shift in his social network. And just as Justin had needed to stop going to certain places (sports bars) so, too, did Greg need to forgo the casino scene. For both of these men, a shift in *who* they spent time with amounted to reaching out for support. For Justin, it meant a return to friends he'd spent less and less time with; for Greg, it meant not seeing his gambling friends at all, since the casino was essentially the only place he met up with them.

Greg's solution was complicated by the fact that he found the casino exciting, so he needed to find some sort of replacement. Inviting other couples over for get-togethers, which worked well for Justin and Amanda, would not work as well for Greg in the long run. He would need something a bit more stimulating to help compensate for the excitement he experienced at the casino and which drew him there.

Greg, Margie, and their counselor brainstormed a list of friends they would like to spend more time with, along with a list of activities they currently enjoy and some new activities they would like to try. The list included bicycling and getting season tickets to the home games of the state university's men's basketball team. Another activity—which was also exciting—was inviting friends over to watch the university's women's basketball games on their large-screen television.

Margie arranged for these events to be alcohol-free by saying that, since everyone would be driving home afterward, she thought it best that they not drink. Everyone accepted this without question. And since she took pleasure in both entertaining and cooking, Margie made these events highly enjoyable for all who came. Greg had a good time as well.

Your Modified Social Network

Consider taking some time now to take stock of your existing social network and to think about ways you might alter it to make it easier for you to move out of the almost alcoholic zone.

You can do this without disclosing your reasons; alternatively, many people say they feel comfortable casually telling friends that they've decided to cut down on their drinking. That explanation is common today and is widely accepted. People today cut back on their drinking just as often as they cut down their intake of fats or carbohydrates, and they don't feel a need to hide that.

The following chart is divided into two columns: friends and family plus activities that *support drinking more*, and friends and family plus activities that *support drinking less.* Re-create this chart in your journal and then identify the people and the activities that belong in each category.

Friends and Family Who Support Drinking More	Friends and Family Who Support Drinking Less
Activities I Engage in with These Friends and Family	Activities I Engage in with These Friends and Family

Your goal now is simple: begin to shift your lifestyle so that you spend more time doing things with friends and family who will make it easier for you to move out of the almost alcoholic zone. Here are some suggestions that others have found helpful in making such a shift:

- You do not necessarily have to totally avoid friends and family who drink more and tend to support heavier drinking. One alternative is to avoid those people in the environments where they drink. In other words, you can invite them to activities that support less drinking or no drinking. It's then up to them to decide whether they want to participate.
- Create interesting activities and make them alcohol-free. Greg and Margie did that when they bought season basketball tickets (no liquor could be served in the university's basketball arena) as well as when they created their basketball home parties.
- Do not simply try to avoid old friends and activities without simultaneously substituting other friends and activities.
- You don't have to make all of these changes overnight. Start with those people and associated activities that most support your drinking and gradually decrease your involvement there while replacing it with people and activities that will make it easier for you to drink less.

By following through with this plan, you are in effect reaching out to others (even if they don't know that!). This plan represents a recognition on your part that the people we choose to spend our time with, along with the activities we choose to participate in, influence our behavior, including how much and how often we drink.

• • •

The point is that a shift in a person's social network—changing who you spend time with socially—can have a powerful effect, in this case on the person's drinking behavior. Again, moving away from a social network that supports almost alcoholic drinking and toward one that does not is a form of reaching out. That is true even if you do not tell anyone that you think you are or may be an almost alcoholic. If you are married or in a relationship, making this shift with mutual support is also a form of reaching out and can help solidify this part of your solution. If for some reason you don't have the support of your spouse or partner or other significant people in your life, this shift will be more difficult, and you will have to reach out beyond this circle for help. Taking an honest look at the consequences of your drinking may help you find the self-motivation to make the extra effort to change—and do it just for yourself.

7

Changing Routines

One thing is unmistakable about human beings: we are creatures of habit. Most of us like our lives to be orderly and do not particularly like unpredictability. We see this trait in children starting at an early age. They love routine and repetition. If you are a parent, you probably know what would happen if, for example, you tried to suddenly alter a bedtime routine: it would be like kicking a hornet's nest. The same thing would happen if you tried to suddenly change the ritual you and your children have established for saying good-bye before they go off to school in the morning. You'd probably agree that it would not be worth the effort.

Routines and Rituals

As adults, we also use routines and rituals to bring structure to our lives and, like children, we can become anxious and upset when they are disrupted or taken away from us. Some routines are positive and helpful, while others can eventually have a negative impact on our lives. To understand just how much we are creatures of habit—for both good and ill—it will help to take stock of some of our own common routines and rituals.

Taking Stock: Personal Routines

Routines are basically habits that we rely upon to structure our day and make life more efficient and predictable, and therefore easier. Think about your daily routines and then answer the following questions:

1. What is your routine for getting up, getting dressed, and getting ready for the day ahead?
2. Is your weekend morning routine different from your weekday routine? If so, how do they differ?
3. What is your routine when you get home from work every day?
4. What routines do you follow when it is time to relax before going to bed?
5. What routines do you follow when it comes to things like cooking, housecleaning, laundry, and gardening?

Most people don't realize just how much their lives are governed by routines until they stop to think about questions like these. More than a few people have laughed when they told us about how they even had very set routines for mowing their lawns!

How do you feel when your routine is disrupted? How much disruption can you tolerate before you will get really upset or irritated? Finally, have you ever had to change a long-standing routine, for example as a result of changing jobs or having a child? Was change easy or difficult for you to make?

Taking Stock: Personal Rituals

Human beings seem hardwired not only to create and stick with routine, but also to do the same with rituals. Again, we see the spontaneous emergence of rituals in young children. They are revealed in small ways, such as the bedtime prayer or good-night kiss, or the hug and "I love you" that's exchanged before they head off to catch the school bus.

No one knows for sure what the exact purposes of rituals are. What we do know is that humans do engage in daily rituals and that without them, people typically get anxious. Of course, sometimes rituals get out of hand and become compulsions, and at their worse are pathological, such as with obsessive-compulsive disorders. Yet even in that form, as with alcohol abuse, they tend to reduce anxiety, at least temporarily.

For most people, rituals and routines combine to form the fabric of day-to-day life. At that level, they help to facilitate, not interfere with, our functionality. Families also have rituals, such as Sunday dinner or Friday pizza-and-movie night. These rituals help families to bond and experience the comfort that can come from being part of a larger group.

Think for a moment about the various rituals in your own life, and then use your journal to answer the following questions:

1. What are the earliest rituals you can remember repeating in your life? What were these rituals? How often did you repeat them? How do you think you would have felt if someone told you to stop a particular ritual?
2. If you have a partner, children, or both, what sorts of daily or weekly rituals do you and they engage in?
3. What personal rituals do you engage in? For example, do you pray? Do you meditate? Do you repeat certain actions before leaving the house for the day? Do you repeat certain actions on returning home?

Routines, Rituals, and Drinking

Men and women who are in recovery from alcoholism or drug addiction are very familiar with the role that rituals and routines played in their lives when they were drinking or using. Here is one such story.

Angie's Story

Now thirty-five, Angie has not had a drink or used pain medication in more than two years. She'd gotten into trouble with both about six years earlier after suffering a back injury in a car crash. Prior to that, she had been a social drinker who enjoyed meeting up with a few other single women for Friday happy hours. She had a steady boyfriend, and both had good jobs and shared many interests. They generally had a very good time together. All things considered, things were looking pretty good for Angie. Then came the car accident.

Afterward, Angie spent ten days in the hospital where she underwent two surgeries on her spine: one in the cervical area and one in the thoracic area. The surgeries were successful to the extent that Angie recovered most of her range of motion and was able to resume her career. She was even able to return to the fitness center she belonged to, where she swam, did light weight workouts, and walked a treadmill. On the other hand, she'd had to give up skiing and jogging.

Although her body was "fixed," to use Angie's word for her surgeries, she nonetheless experienced chronic pain in her back and neck. The pain seemed to correlate with stress, so if Angie was having a tough work week filled with deadlines, her back and neck would ache at night. She was given pain medicine—lots of it—and encouraged to use it liberally. "At the time," she explained, "a lot of doctors believed that the pain medication they were dispensing was not addicting."

About three months after her accident and surgeries, Angie's boyfriend told her over the phone that he had decided he needed some "space." Angie felt her stomach sink as he explained that he thought they should "take a break" from their relationship. "I knew very well what he was saying," Angie explained. "He was trying to sugarcoat it, but we were breaking up, plain and simple." What made Angie angry as well as upset, she said, was that her boyfriend had chosen to break up over the phone. "He couldn't even take five minutes to face me in person!" she said.

After the breakup, Angie started drinking more—more often and more heavily. To make a long story short, within a year she was addicted to pain medication and was well into the almost alcoholic zone in her drinking behavior. She described the fairly elaborate rituals and routines that she had built around her use of both medication and alcohol: "I was at the point where my life had begun to revolve around my pills and my wine," she said, adding, "You could definitely say that I had a commitment to both, though technically I was not yet an alcoholic because I would not go into withdrawal on the few occasions I tried, unsuccessfully, to stop."

Angie described how she would go to the bathroom at work, at precise four-hour intervals, to take a pain pill. "I even bought this fancy little clock that I kept on my desk to keep track of the time. I had a polishing cloth in my desk and I would take it out first thing every morning and polish the clock. I also kept spare batteries in my desk, and I checked every few days using my computer to make sure that the clock was keeping precisely the right time."

Angie went on: "I had slowed down on my exercise, and when I did go to the club, I'd make sure my time there would never interfere with my four-hour pain pill schedule. Even if I went to a movie, I'd always make sure that the movie schedule would not interfere with it!"

Each day when she got home from work, Angie would engage in drinking rituals and routines. "I'd started buying my wine by the case. Every day when I got home, the first thing I'd do was count my bottles of wine. I'd also make sure there was always a spare bottle cooling in the fridge. When I was down to three bottles, that was time to call and order another case. The wine store would deliver free if you ordered a case, and it would be outside my front door when I got home the next day."

Another ritual and routine was associated with Angie's drinking: "I had my favorite wine glass and also several backups, wrapped in paper and stored in a closet, in case the one I was using broke. That happened more than once, because I was drinking several glasses of wine a night—and that was on top of my pain pills. I'd pour that first glass with such anticipation! Then I'd turn on the news and sit on the couch and drink. I would drink exactly two glasses of wine before having dinner—again while watching television."

• • •

Once again, we are creatures of habit, and that extends to drinking. It isn't difficult to see how Angie's drinking (and use of pain medication) was supported by her rituals and routines. Her solution to moving out of the almost alcoholic zone (and she was in pretty deep!) would require changing those rituals and routines.

Personal Drinking Rituals and Routines

Using your journal, take a moment to describe the rituals and routines that you have built around drinking, using the following questions as food for thought:

1. Looking back on the past several years, in what ways have your daily routines changed to accommodate drinking? In particular, have you given up any activities in order to drink?
2. Have you developed a habit of drinking starting at a certain hour? Are you careful not to schedule another activity during this time?
3. Do you have a favorite form of liquor, wine, or beer that you look forward to drinking? Are you careful to make sure that your supply does not run low?

QUESTIONS CONTINUED ON NEXT PAGE

4. Do you, as Angie did, have a favorite glass that you drink from?

5. Is your drinking associated with any rituals, such as changing into comfortable clothes, turning on the television or music, or sitting in a certain place?

6. If you have a family, has your family grown accustomed to accommodating your drinking routines? For example, if you have children, do they know not to disturb you when you are drinking? If you have a partner, does he or she know not to disturb your drinking routine?

Breaking Old Habits

Anyone who has tried to break an old habit knows that it doesn't happen effortlessly. Yet, although difficult, research has shown that it does get easier with time and that the first ninety days are the most critical to changing old habits. In other words, if you can sustain a change for ninety days, it gets easier to sustain it permanently after that. This applies to virtually any habit, even one that is addicting, such as cigarette smoking. For example, consider a smoker who is in the habit of smoking that first cigarette half an hour after getting up in the morning, while drinking a cup of coffee at the kitchen table. Now, say that same smoker decides to change that routine by getting into his car and getting his coffee at a drive-through before lighting that first cigarette. Now, *if* he can do this for ninety days, he will probably be able to drop his old routine completely. Moreover, this one change in routine can mark the beginning of stopping smoking altogether.

• • •

Now, let's look at Angie and how she altered her daily routines and rituals in order to help herself move out of the almost alcoholic zone. This was a very important part of the solution for her—just as important as building a support network. She began this work soon after deciding that she should seek some counseling. As is true for the majority of almost alcoholics, Angie's stated reason for coming to see the counselor was that she was feeling depressed and unhappy. Her life, she explained to the counselor, seemed to have been going downhill ever since she had the car accident. She had, for example, to cope with chronic pain. She took medication for this, she explained, and while it helped relieve the pain, it left her feeling chronically groggy. "I feel like I'm living in a fog," she told the counselor.

Angie said that she'd also been feeling down ever since her boyfriend broke up with her. Lately she'd been thinking that she would never realize her dream of meeting Mr. Right, getting married, and having a family.

The counselor could well understand how Angie could be feeling depressed. However, as the counselor got to know Angie better, she began to suspect that drinking in combination with chronic use of pain medication was a major issue underlying Angie's unhappiness. The counselor shared this thought with Angie and asked for her reaction. Angie said it was true that her drinking had increased significantly and that on a couple of occasions when she had tried to stop taking the medication, she had felt "miserable." The counselor explained that what Angie experienced on those occasions were most likely symptoms of opiate withdrawal, since the pain medication Angie had been taking all this time was in fact classified as an opiate—similar in its action to heroin. In addition, drinking as much alcohol as she did very likely contributed to Angie's depression.

Angie was shocked by what the counselor was telling her and said she needed to think about it. When she returned for her next counseling session, she reported that she had indeed reflected on her drinking as well as her use of pain medication and had decided that both would have to change somehow if she was to "stop being bogged down and get on with my life." In essence, Angie did have a vision for her life and was choosing to pursue it again.

Angie's Solution

Before we look at Angie's rituals and routines, let's look at her social network. Since she drank mostly alone and had drifted away from her small circle of friends, Angie's issue was not that she spent a lot of time with people who promoted drinking, but rather that she had become socially isolated. None of her friends were more than social drinkers, and although she stayed in touch with them via phone and e-mail, she had seen less and less of them over the previous year. Therefore, one part of her solution would be to reconnect with her friends and spend more face-to-face time with them. In talking it through with her counselor, though, Angie decided that meeting at happy hours would not be the best forum for doing this. So instead she told her friends that she was embarking on a program to get back into physical shape and that part of that was no drinking. She did not disclose that she believed she had a drinking problem or explain how long she intended to stop drinking. Her friends simply accepted Angie's decision and arranged to get together in other ways, such as taking a bike ride or meeting at the fitness club they belonged to for a swim followed by low-calorie smoothies.

Angie's solution had two benefits. First, it helped to relieve her isolation and move her toward a social network that would support not drinking. Second, it represented a step toward breaking up the routines and rituals that supported her almost alcoholic drinking behavior.

Angie didn't stop there, however. After discussing the role that routines and rituals serve in maintaining almost alcoholic drinking, Angie and her counselor came up with a plan to change the routines and rituals that surrounded her drinking. That plan included the following:

- Returning to the fitness center three times a week right after work instead of going home and drinking
- Meeting with one or more friends for coffee after work once a week instead of going home and drinking
- Getting rid of her favorite wine glasses
- Preparing dinner while drinking some juice and watching the evening news instead of sitting on the couch and drinking
- Stopping buying wine by the case

Angie did not totally stop drinking, although she did stop totally for the ninety days that her counselor recommended. She also worked with her doctors to wean herself off the pain medication. Instead of using the medication for her pain, she signed up for lessons in meditation, which has been found to help relieve pain, along with weekly massages for the same reason. Six months later, she was a woman who had regained her physical condition and stamina. She had also restored her circle of friends and had cautiously begun dating again, protecting herself, she said, by not allowing her expectations to get too high. "I'm open to dating a new man once a week," she explained. "It seems I can always tell within an hour if a man is someone I'd be interested in seeing again. If I am, and he calls me back, I'll see him again. But I won't pursue him. I definitely want to be pursued!"

So Angie had taken back control of her life and had taken her first steps toward realizing her vision of a happy life. One year after starting therapy, she was someone who might have a glass of wine over dinner on a date or at a Friday afternoon happy hour with friends. She no longer drank at home at all. She was drug free. And she had even added a new ritual to her life: each weekday morning before leaving for work, she would take a minute or two to read from one of two daily meditation books she'd found at a local bookstore.

Finding Your Solution

On a scale of 1 to 10, with 10 meaning *most willing*, how willing are you today to take steps to change your rituals and routines? If you score a 5 or higher, you are probably ready to try some things that will support your decision to change your drinking behavior. A score of lower than 5 means that you're unsure about your readiness to change, and you might want to go back and review chapters 2 through 4 before moving on. If you think you're ready to change, take out your journal and try the next exercise.

You can use the chart below to think about and then plan how you would like to modify your current routines and daily rituals to support your decision to move out of the almost alcoholic zone.

After giving some thought to the changes you'd like to make, write them down in your journal. Keep in mind that it is much easier to drop a routine or ritual if we add a new one in its place. In contrast, it can be very difficult to change a habit without substituting a new one.

Current Daily Routines	Substitute Daily Routines
Current Daily Rituals	Substitute Daily Rituals

In chapter 5, we talked about the importance of a personal inventory—taking an honest look at the man or woman in the mirror and the role that drinking has played in your life. Chapter 6 was about building a social network that supports your decision to change your drinking behaviors. This chapter has offered a third solution for the almost alcoholic: to alter the routines and rituals that supported almost alcoholic drinking and replace them with new ones that support a decision to change. In chapter 8, we'll look at the importance of developing refusal skills to protect yourself in drinking situations. Keep in mind, as you go through this second part of the book, that the solutions we are offering are *cumulative*. In other words, they will work best if you pursue all of them. They are all based on research and are methods that have been shown to be effective in helping individuals change their drinking behavior.

8

Developing Refusal Skills

Many people say that one of the most difficult situations they face when they're trying to move out of the almost alcoholic zone is saying no when a friend or family member offers them a drink. These people will likely be accustomed to you being a drinking person, although they will probably not think of you as having a "drinking problem." Accordingly, they will expect you to want a drink and will naturally offer you one or suggest you have one together.

Of course, the easiest and perhaps best way to not drink is to avoid putting yourself in situations where you will feel pressured to do so. Office parties, happy hours, and even some business meetings are situations in which drinking is very common and your motivation to change may be tested. The same thing may apply to backyard barbecues or meeting friends at a sports bar or someone's house to watch a game.

Some people who've made a decision to stop drinking, or who've cut back because their drinking patterns put them somewhere in the almost alcoholic gray zone, say that they avoid such situations as much as possible. Some, as described earlier, substitute activities that are fun but do not include drinking as part of the scene. However, even though you may have committed yourself to a modified lifestyle in order to support your decision, the reality is that you may not be able to avoid every situation where drinking occurs. For that reason, it's best to know how to say "no thanks" in a way that is effective but does not offend others or open up more discussion about your drinking than you'd prefer.

The method described in this chapter is supported by research on how to help people overcome shyness or social anxiety and become more assertive. Many people fit that description, and you may be one of them. The technique, which is broken down into four steps, is designed to help you "find your voice."

Building Refusal Skills

We've been told more than a few times that while saying no to a drink may be hard at first, it gets easier with practice. Research has shown that a technique called "cognitive role playing" can be extremely helpful in developing social skills like saying no. It also helps reduce people's anxiety when they have to practice the skill in a real—as oppose to an imagined—situation.

To practice refusal skills, follow these four steps:

1. Identify difficult situations.
2. Choose your refusal repertoire.
3. Practice.
4. Implement.

Step 1: Identify Difficult Situations

How difficult a situation is can vary a great deal for each individual. Anyone wanting to refuse a drink might be severely tested during happy hour at a tavern. Some other situations may be just as challenging, if not more so, for some people yet be handled with ease by others. One woman who'd decided to stop drinking for a while as a first step in leaving the almost alcoholic zone explained that a long-standing ritual that she and her husband had developed during their twenty-five years of marriage could be her most challenging situation. That ritual involved sitting together in comfortable chairs on a screened-in porch that overlooked a flower garden and sharing a cocktail. For Christine that ritual had evolved, over years and due to a number of factors, into drinking in an almost alcoholic way.

Christine had considered abandoning this ritual altogether as part of her solution but decided in the end that she did not want to do that. This time together with her husband was too valuable to her. For his part, although he agreed that Christine would do well to cut down on her drinking, he did not see anything wrong with their cocktail hour. Therefore, Christine would have to think of a way to say no that would not lead to conflict while avoiding her old pattern of almost alcoholic drinking that most often began with cocktail hour. And she did not want to get into a long discussion with her husband about it, as she expected he would only try to persuade her to have that cocktail. "John is a wonderful husband," Christine explained, "but he hasn't had my experience with drinking and he doesn't really understand how difficult it has become for me to stop after one cocktail, because he has no trouble doing so."

Christine's story illustrates a problem you are likely to face: refusing an invitation to drink in a situation when someone doesn't understand your almost alcoholic drinking, doesn't see the risks involved for you in that situation, or isn't aware of your decision to change.

To begin developing your refusal skills, take some time to identify several situations, like those described so far (examples of which are given below), in which you would feel pressure to take a drink instead of saying no. In your journal, make two columns: one labeled *physical context,* in which you'll list where you would be, and one labeled *social context,* in which you'll list who you would be with.

Physical Context	**Social Context**
1. Happy hour in a bar __________ __________ __________	With co-workers, two of whom are also regular drinking buddies __________ __________ __________
2. Restaurant in a strange city __________ __________ __________	With clients I'm wining and dining __________ __________ __________

Step 2: Choose Your Refusal Repertoire

Some of the people we've worked with have shared how they were able to say no in various situations. Many of these choices are rather creative. Here are a few examples:

- Sharon, a pediatric nurse, had decided several years earlier to stop drinking for two reasons: she had developed type 2 diabetes and, after thinking about it carefully, she'd concluded that her almost alcoholic drinking pattern had contributed greatly to a long-standing depression. Once fairly isolated, Sharon now had a large circle of friends, many of whom did not drink at all and none of whom were almost alcoholics. Nevertheless, Sharon frequently found herself in a situation where someone offered her a drink. Sharon told us that her stock reply at such times was this: "Thanks, but I drank my whole life's quota of alcohol by the time I was forty, so I'll pass." Many people, Sharon said, responded to this with a smile or a laugh. No one, she said, ever frowned or pressed her to take a drink.
- Mitch, an engineer, had made several decisions about his drinking, including never drinking at home and not meeting with friends for happy hours, as he once had every Friday after work. He would, however, allow himself one beer when he occasionally met friends at a sports bar to watch the local college's basketball games. After that beer, he drank soda. Whenever someone offered Mitch another beer or ask why he was drinking soda, Mitch would respond: "My doctor told me I had to cut down. High cholesterol and borderline diabetes. It's either that or medication." Just as Sharon experienced, no one ever challenged Mitch when he said that.

- Gloria, a financial adviser, repeatedly offered this simple refusal: "I need to watch my weight. No one wants to talk to a fat financial adviser!" That's what she'd say whenever someone offered her a second drink.
- Oscar had decided that he'd become an almost alcoholic and opted to abstain for ninety days as a first step in his solution. His response to friends when he was in a drinking situation was straightforward without revealing too much. He'd say, "I decided to stop drinking for a while. I'm looking to improve my health for the years ahead and drinking is one of the things I'm looking at." Friends accepted this, especially because Oscar also talked about how he was modifying his eating and exercising habits (which were other parts of his solution).

• • •

Feel free to use any of these ideas, modify them, or come up with your own creative reasons to refuse a drink. Then make a list of responses in your journal under the heading "Refusal Statements." You can add to it whenever you think of new, creative ways to say no.

Step 3: Practice!

This is the step in developing refusal skills that sometimes strikes people as silly at first, yet research strongly supports its effectiveness. The role playing that's involved is an effective way to bridge the gap between *thinking* and *doing*—between identifying situations and coming up with a refusal repertoire, and actually doing it. Here is how to get started:

- Bring a list of your refusal statments with you.

- Find a quiet place where you will not be interrupted for at least fifteen minutes.
- Place two chairs a few feet apart, facing each other, and sit in one of the chairs.
- Imagine that someone is sitting in the other chair and has just said to you, "How about a drink?"
- Say *out loud*, to the imaginary person facing you, one of your refusal statements.
- Repeat the last two steps, using a different refusal statement each time. Again, be sure to say it out loud and address the empty chair and the imaginary person in front of you.
- Practice saying each refusal statement twice.

For best results, repeat the above exercise once a day for at least ten days.

Most people who follow through with this step conscientiously report that they do indeed get more comfortable repeating their refusal statements, not only in this role-play situation but in real life as well.

Step 4: Implement!

Congratulations—you're almost there! The fourth and final step in developing refusal skills is to begin using them in real situations. Working through steps 1 through 3 makes it easier for most people to use refusal statements when situations arise. We hope that is true for you.

Even with lots of practice, though, you may still experience some discomfort the first few times you use your refusal skills. Our best advice is not to let this discourage you, for two reasons. First, it *will* get easier the more you practice. Second, you will likely have to use your refusal skills only once or twice with any one person. Those people who are truly your friends, as well as people who simply have good manners, will respect your refusal without difficulty. On the other hand, those who do not may be people you should think about avoiding.

Dealing with Persistent Invitations to Drink

Although the strategy we've described will work in most cases, it can be useful to anticipate a more difficult situation, namely, one in which a friend pushes you to drink even after you've given a refusal. If this happens, this person is usually either a regular drinking companion of yours and/or someone with a drinking problem of his or her own. The person may be insistent or may offer to pay for your drinks. In the worst-case scenario, he or she may go so far as to tease or ridicule you for not drinking.

Our first recommendation in such situations is to repeat the reason you've already stated for not drinking, *but more forcefully*, for example:

- "I told you that I am not drinking these days as part of my plan to get in better shape and take care of my health. I'll let you know if that changes."
- "My doctor has advised me to stay away from alcohol so we can monitor my health to see if drinking could be causing me a problem. I'm sticking with that advice."
- "I decided to stop drinking to see if that can be a way for me not to need medication, and that's what I'm going to do."

Statements such as the above can be a good fallback and we advise you to practice them out loud, just as you practiced your refusal repertoire. In the unlikely event that even these do not cause someone to drop the issue of your drinking, you may want to give some thought to just how much that person respects you and your right to make decisions for yourself. You may decide that it's necessary to avoid or severely limit your contact with that person.

• • •

By now your solution for exiting the almost alcoholic zone should be taking shape. The combination of self-reflection, lifestyle changes, and effective refusal skills can form the foundation for the change you want to make. In the next two chapters, we will be looking at another dimension of the solution: your emotions and the role they play both in drinking and in not drinking in an almost alcoholic way.

9

Coping with Loneliness and Boredom

The elderly, defined as men and women age sixty and older, are now the fastest growing segment of the population in the United States and many other countries, and they will continue to be so for many years. Among this group, 15 percent of men and 12 percent of women report having more than one drink every day. Survey results of patients seen in various health care settings show an increasing prevalence of alcohol use and abuse among this population. Meanwhile, in acute care hospitals, older adults are admitted for alcohol-related issues at about the same rate as they are admitted for cardiac problems. Even more startling, the number of nursing home residents thought to be "problem drinkers" has been estimated as high as 49 percent.[22]

A Vulnerable Population

The title of this chapter helps explain why older Americans (as well as older citizens elsewhere) are so vulnerable to excess drinking (and to becoming almost alcoholics). Here is an example.

Ethan's and Mary's Stories

Although they lived in the same town and occasionally attended the same senior center, Ethan and Mary did not know one another well. Both were in their late sixties and widowed. Ethan lived in a condo in an over-fifty-five community that he and his late wife had moved into after they retired. After her husband died, Mary sold the home they had lived in for some fifty years and moved into an assisted-living facility. She had a modest but comfortable one-bedroom unit. It included a kitchenette, though Mary took most of her meals in a common dining area.

Ethan and Mary both had grown children but they understood that, like everyone else they knew, their children were more than busy running their own lives. Ethan had two married sons, whom he spoke with weekly but saw infrequently. His older son, Tyler, was an engineer and had already moved his family several times in pursuit of his career. Tyler currently lived with his own two sons and wife one state away. It was about a four-hour drive, so Ethan saw Tyler and his family mostly on holidays. Fortunately, Ethan was in good health and still quite mobile, so he was able to make the trip without difficulty.

Ethan's other son, Will, was a schoolteacher who lived nearby with his family. However, Will and his wife were quite busy with their own four children, including a girl who'd been diagnosed as autistic and who required extra care from them.

Ethan usually spent alternate holidays with his sons and their families and was able to attend some of events of his grandchildren who lived in his town, including some of his granddaughter's lacrosse games and his grandsons' soccer games. He also enjoyed being invited to their birthday parties.

Despite a hectic schedule, Will made a point of visiting with Ethan once a week. In good weather, they'd sit on a small deck outside Ethan's condo and share a beer. What Will didn't know was that his father would have two, three, or even four more beers after he left and that this had been Ethan's drinking habit now for several years. He'd recently been diagnosed with acid reflux and his cholesterol level was high enough to require medication. During those office visits, Ethan had not disclosed to his doctor how much he drank.

Mary liked her little apartment in the assisted-living center well enough, though she found the various activities it hosted to be less interesting that she'd initially hoped. For one thing, they were mostly attended by men and women ten years or more her senior. Although she could foresee a time when she might "fit in" better, for now she was mostly bored with them. To compensate, she'd decided to try out the town's senior center, where she discovered a "younger" crowd. It was there that she met Ethan. Looking for something to do, they both had signed up to help out with the town's annual budget referendums and with monthly potluck luncheons that raised money for the center's lending library. Even taken together, however, these activities occupied only a small fraction of their time.

After she had a light dinner, Mary would retire to her small apartment for the evening, where she would almost always pour herself two or three glasses of wine. She'd sip these while watching television or reading a book until it was time to go to bed. Although some might consider this "no big deal," Mary had survived a bout with breast cancer twenty years earlier and, although she remained in remission, the amount she was drinking increased her risk of a recurrence of either breast cancer or cancer in another organ. In addition, Mary's doctor had called her after her last yearly physical to inform her that blood tests had detected a "slight" problem with her liver. He'd advised her to "cut down" on her drinking to no more than one glass of wine a day. Again, research has shown that it takes less time and lower doses of alcohol to cause liver damage in women; thus, Mary was putting herself in double jeopardy by drinking as much as she did.

Ethan and Mary had more in common than their age or loss of spouses. They shared something that millions of older men and women can readily relate to: loneliness and boredom. And it was those emotions that promoted their drinking behavior.[23]

Not Just the Elderly

The elderly are not the only group in the population vulnerable to loneliness and boredom and, therefore, to drinking beyond the normal social level. Because boredom and loneliness appear to spring from isolation, anyone who leads a life characterized by isolation is more vulnerable to becoming an almost alcoholic. In our experience, people who are at risk due to isolation and its effects include the following:

- Widowed men and women
- The elderly
- Single parents
- People with a disabling illness
- People suffering from depression
- People who are exceptionally shy or suffer from social anxiety

- The long-term unemployed

Although men and women in the above situations may recognize that they are somewhat isolated, often they don't realize that they drink in an effort to ward off boredom and loneliness. In other words, they don't "connect the dots" between their isolation, the boredom and loneliness it creates, and their drinking behavior. This is similar to how people who are almost alcoholics will seek counseling for depression, insomnia, or marital conflict and not see the connection between any of those problems and their drinking.

Overcoming Isolation, Loneliness, and Boredom

Take a few minutes now and reflect on your current circumstances in your journal. Then respond to the following exercises:

Re-create the following scale in your journal, and put an "I" at the point that, in your opinion, most accurately reflects how *isolated* you are from others.

	Not at All			Somewhat			Extremely		
1	2	3	4	5	6	7	8	9	10

Now, put an "L" at the point on the scale that, in your opinion, most accurately reflects how *lonely* you feel on a day-to-day basis.

Finally, put a "B" at the point on the scale that, in your opinion, most accurately reflects how *bored* you feel on a day-to-day basis.

Isolation, and the loneliness and boredom it creates, is unpleasant for everyone. However, for almost alcoholics who want to leave that drinking zone and who have developed a pattern of drinking to compensate for loneliness and/or boredom, isolation can be a major stumbling block. If your score on any of the scales is 6 or higher, this may be an issue that should be addressed in your solution. If all your scores clustered in the 6 to 10 range, then you are particularly vulnerable to almost alcoholic drinking as way to escape from or medicate your discomfort and unhappiness. Here is how one person dealt with isolation while working to change his drinking behavior.

Frank's Story

Frank, a forty-one-year-old retired veteran who'd enlisted at eighteen, had become an almost alcoholic during the three years since he left active duty. Married with two sons, Frank had taken a job with a company that handled security for retail stores and shopping malls. Between that and his veteran's benefits, Frank and his family were financially secure. The income that his wife earned as a licensed practical nurse had gone into college funds for the boys, home improvements, and a nice vacation fund.

As a youth, Frank had never been a very social person. He had a small circle of friends and he hung out with them through high school. After enlisting, he pretty much lost contact with this group. In the service, meanwhile, he got along well but was not really "buddies" with anyone. The family moved with him twice during his years in the service, when the boys were very young. After that, they bought a home in the community where Frank had grown up and settled down while he went on more tours of duty. He did his job well, earning two medals for outstanding service—including one for valor on the battlefield—and receiving several promotions.

In the social environment that defines the military, Frank functioned well. Although he had no best friend, he was not unfriendly, and although he hung out with his fellow servicemen much less than almost anyone else he knew, he did make a point of attending certain social events. What he looked forward to the most were his leaves, when he'd return home to be with his wife and boys.

It was after retiring from the service that Frank started drinking more than ever before. His boys, by then in their late teens, spent less and less time at home. His wife continued to work full time and loved her job. Frank, meanwhile, found his new security work dull. He supervised a staff of ten security officers for a midsize shopping mall. He would walk the mall himself every day but spent most of his time in an office, overseeing work schedules, glancing at security cameras, and filling out paperwork in response to reports of shoplifting.

Eventually, Frank's drinking increased to the point where he kept a bottle of bourbon in his desk drawer at work. He did not open it every day, yet that bottle of bourbon eventually led him to seek counseling.

Shortly before Frank was scheduled to head home one day, his supervisor, whom he usually met with only once a month, abruptly appeared in his office. Their interaction was brief and blunt: a store owner had reported smelling alcohol on Frank's breath. Frank's boss made it clear that Frank had only two choices: get rid of his bottle and never drink on the job again or quit. There would be no second chance.

When Frank told his wife, Cindy, about the incident, she admitted that she, too, had detected the smell of alcohol on Frank's breath on several occasions when he got home from work. She hadn't brought it up for fear of embarrassing him.

The confrontation with his boss, along with Cindy's subsequent comment, was enough to convince Frank that he needed to do something about his drinking. The first thing he did was to get rid of the bourbon bottle. He'd resolved to never take a drink at work again. At home, however, Frank continued to drink—albeit beer instead of bourbon. At the same time he found himself slipping deeper and deeper into a state of depression. Cindy noticed that Frank wasn't himself; he had progressively lost interest in maintaining the house and its lawn and gardens. Never a talkative sort, he nevertheless seemed to become ever more withdrawn. It pained her to see him like that. Always one who held her husband in high esteem, Cindy finally broke down and spoke her mind. "I found myself watching this man I loved, this brave, strong, and responsible husband and father," she explained, "slowly withering before my eyes." She convinced Frank to talk to his doctor and went with him to the appointment. The doctor spent half an hour with them and then referred Frank to a therapist he said he knew personally and had high regard for.

It did not take the therapist long to figure out that, in addition to drinking, boredom was a major issue for Frank, along with the social isolation he experienced since retiring from the service. The therapist asked Frank questions very similar to the ones presented earlier in this chapter. He then set out to work collaboratively with Frank on developing the following solutions.

Reestablishing Friendships

The development of the Internet and, more recently, the popularity of social media sites like Facebook have created unprecedented opportunity for people to connect (and reconnect) with each other. Although Frank was computer literate and used the Internet regularly to shop, review products, and even read the news, he'd never looked into any of the social media sites. With some encouragement and coaching from his counselor, however, Frank created a personal Facebook page and also joined a community website for veterans.

Though shy by nature, Frank found it relatively easy to reach out through the Internet. Within a month or so, he'd established communication with several high school friends who, he learned, still lived in the area. He also was contacted by several fellow retired veterans who lived nearby.

What started out as an exchange of e-mail eventually led to face-to-face contacts, and Frank began to build a circle of friends connected by shared experiences. He and Cindy even attended a "mini-reunion" of his local classmates from high school, who had maintained an informal network over the years.

Community Involvement

A second part of Frank's solution for ending his isolation was to get involved in his community, and again the Internet played a role. Frank had always enjoyed good health and had suffered only minor injuries during his combat duty. For years he had exercised regularly and watched his weight, and although he'd slacked off somewhat as he started drinking more, he was still in great shape.

During a church service one day, Frank's minister spoke about families in the community who were dealing with serious, sometimes even terminal illnesses, including a couple in their own congregation. The pastor mentioned a website that was dedicated to creating local caregiving "networks" to help such families with anything from child care to shopping to cleaning house for someone who was bedridden. This idea of communities coming together to take care of their own struck a chord in Frank.

When Frank got home that Sunday, he fired up his computer and quickly found the website his minister had mentioned. He also learned that two caregiving networks already existed in his community, one of which was dedicated to helping the family of a man about Frank's age who was dealing with colon cancer. Frank entered his name as a volunteer and was quickly accepted. He decided that one way he could help was to become part of a three-member team that cared for the family's lawn, including regular mowing and periodic cleanups.

In time, Frank got to know a number of men and women who were part of caretaking networks in his community. Cindy also signed up and together they eventually made several new friends who became part of their new social network.

Developing New Interests

Between his expanded social network and community service, Frank had moved a long way from his state of isolation. He no longer felt the weight of boredom on his shoulders. He kept the same job, but he did not feel lonely anymore when he walked the halls of the shopping mall. He even ran into people he knew now and then and paused to chat for a minute or two.

That helped Frank a great deal and was a plus in the eyes of many store managers, who wanted their environment to be consumer friendly. In time Frank was able to reduce his drinking significantly; he now had an occasional beer or two on the weekend, always in a social context. Most important, he no longer felt an urge to drink. Still, that is not where Frank stopped.

Through his Internet contacts, Frank learned about another organization—the Wounded Warrior Project.[24] This national nonprofit and nonpolitical organization advocates for the needs of veterans wounded in action as well as those who suffer from a mental illness such as post-traumatic stress disorder (PTSD) as a result of the stress of combat or repeated tours of duty. Grateful that he had avoided such a fate himself, Frank joined this group and participated as time allowed. He wrote letters to government officials, helped organize fund-raisers, and spoke as part of panels of veterans at various events intended to raise public awareness about the needs of wounded veterans.

• • •

Taken together, these three areas of activity—establishing and renewing friendships, becoming involved in the community, and developing new interests—formed a solution for Frank's isolation and the role it had played in his almost alcoholic drinking. Although the specifics of any individual's social networking, community involvement, and other activities can vary a great deal, it is these *themes* that are important.

Next we will look at how resentment, anger, and stress can play a role in almost alcoholic drinking.

10

Coping with Anger, Resentment, and Stress

"For a long time I drank in order to find the courage to speak my mind and, if necessary, tell someone off!" said Jamal. Therein lies a major trap for many almost alcoholics. It's a trap they need to learn how to avoid, lest they remain stuck in the almost alcoholic zone.

Fight or Flight: Part of Being Human

Scientists have long agreed that humans, like countless other species, are hardwired with what is called a "fight or flight" instinct. Faced with danger, we are programmed to do one of two things: flee the threat or fight the threat. Most of us are rarely faced with actual physical threats to our survival. It's true that men and women in the armed forces may find themselves in combat theaters and people affected by crime or natural disasters certainly face such threats, but for the vast majority of us, the "threats" we face are more psychological than mortal.

We feel "threatened" for example, when we are treated in any of the following ways:

- When someone treats us with contempt or disrespect
- When someone criticizes us harshly
- When we are demeaned or patronized by others
- When someone directs sarcasm at us
- When someone denigrates our competence or abilities

Nature appears to have programmed most species faced with threats to react first with *flight* in an effort to escape. Failing that, if we are cornered, we are programmed to *fight.*

Have you experienced any of the above? Most humans experience all of the above at one time or another. If you are lucky, these experiences are relatively rare. But what about Jamal, who says he drank to find the courage to fight? As he described it, he was raised by a very critical father and a passive mother. Jamal portrayed his father as someone who was not only critical, in the sense of finding fault, but actually demeaning. "He'd call me stupid all the time," Jamal said. "If I made a mistake, he'd laugh at me, and not in a very kind way. It was like I could never screw up just by accident—every mistake I made was because I was incompetent."

One of the areas that Jamal excelled in as a teen was baseball, and he made the high school varsity team. Although he loved to play, he hated it when his father would show up for a game. "He'd sit in the bleachers and shake his head in disgust if I struck out or made a bad throw." Jamal's father's attitude affected Jamal so much that his coach finally pulled his father aside and confronted him. "After that he stopped showing up at games," Jamal said. "We didn't talk about baseball after that. I didn't tell him when I did well or even when our team won the state championship. I just knew he wouldn't have anything good to say."

Jamal had learned to suppress his anger starting at an early age. Even as a young child, he didn't dare respond to his father's sarcasm or criticism, as he knew he would then have to endure a withering round of ridicule and perhaps physical punishment. It isn't hard to understand why Jamal would suppress his anger. Faced with a hostile father, Jamal experienced regular urges to flee, to run away from home. In reality, he knew this was not a realistic option. And to make matters worse, on several occasions his father—as though reading Jamal's mind—actually brought it up. "Anytime you want to leave here," he'd say, "just let me know. I'll even give you a suitcase and fifty bucks."

As an adult, Jamal suffered from extremely low self-esteem. He was bright and did well in school. His father refused to pay, so he'd put himself through college while working full time in a food market. It was part of a large chain, and over time Jamal worked his way up through the ranks, starting off as a stocking clerk and cashier to his current position as an assistant manager of a store that did millions of dollars a year in business. Still, in his personal life he did not hold himself in high esteem. That was one reason he'd been stuck in an assistant manager position for five years when several others who had similar experience and even lesser performance ratings were now managers.

Outwardly, two things about Jamal's personality stood in his way, and they were related. First, he was socially very shy.

He found company functions to be painful, and he knew he was not as comfortable chatting with his employees as he should be given his position. Second, he hated confrontation and avoided it as much as possible. Both of these interpersonal handicaps were the result of his relationship with his father.

At home, Jamal tended to be quiet and unassuming. Married for twenty years, with a son and daughter, he was undemanding, thoughtful, mild-mannered, and generous—except when he drank. It was alcohol, he explained, that "unleashes the demon in me."

Jamal did not drink every day, nor did he get angry every day. Even so, as he looked back on his life, he could see a pattern that had started in his early twenties. That pattern went like this:

- Jamal would feel insulted or hurt about something. It would not take much to hurt his feelings. An offhand remark by a co-worker, a slight criticism (intended to be constructive) from his boss, or a touch of sarcasm or anger from his wife or one of his children would be enough to wound him emotionally.
- Jamal would stuff his anger. Over time—weeks, even months—he would bury his angry feelings. No one looking at or interacting with him would suspect that these feelings were lurking under the surface.
- Jamal would drink—more than normal social drinking. And sometimes he would drink to the point where alcohol would disinhibit his pent-up anger enough and it would come out. At such times, Jamal admitted to a counselor, he probably sounded a lot like his father.

All of this came out in marriage counseling after Jamal had exploded at his wife and children often enough that she told him she was beginning to lose her trust in him and to doubt his love for her. Neither Jamal nor his wife thought he was an alcoholic. His wife, though, had made the connection between Jamal's drinking and his angry outbursts.

Emotional Wounds and Suppressed Anger

Jamal is a good example of someone who was wounded as a child and had little choice but to bear those wounds, because fleeing was not an option. As a child and teen, he dared not give voice to the hurt or anger he felt. As an adult, he still kept these emotions bottled up. He was socially shy and unassertive. But he found that drinking could help him overcome his inhibitions and allow him to voice his anger. Of course, beneath that anger was a lot of emotional pain—a virtual reservoir of pain that had collected over many years.

Jamal's shyness and lack of assertiveness resulted from his very low self-esteem. Here's the way he put it, describing his self-image growing up: "I would tell myself that I did not deserve happiness or joy; I would tell myself I deserved sadness." According to Jamal, such a statement about himself was the only way he could make sense of his experience a child.

• • •

Suppressing anger caused by emotional wounds inevitably leads not only to a damaged self-image, but also to resentment. And Jamal did harbor resentment—toward all those who hurt his feelings. If his wife inadvertently said or did something that bothered him, he'd never address it directly. But he'd certainly remember it while suppressing his hurt and anger. He would feel resentment, and that resentment would come out at some point, after he'd had enough to drink. Then he'd accuse his wife of not caring about him or of disrespecting him. Sometimes he'd even drop hints that he was thinking about leaving. These veiled threats represented yet another example of the flight reflex we all share. In this case, Jamal fantasized about fleeing his marriage rather than addressing the things that bothered him. The latter, of course, is more comparable to fighting than to fleeing.

Breaking the Anger-Resentment-Drinking Connection

Turning to alcohol in an effort to "anesthetize" emotions, in particular pain and anger, was not something unique to Jamal. Historically, alcohol was used for just that purpose. Prior to the development of modern anesthetics, for example, alcohol was routinely given to patients prior to surgery (as was cocaine!). Alcohol has a numbing effect, and people like Jamal, who have learned to suppress emotional pain and anger, end up carrying around a lot of unexpressed resentment. And that resentment makes them more likely to trying to numb all of these feelings by drinking. That is exactly what Jamal did. Although he was not a daily drinker or an alcoholic, Jamal was an almost alcoholic by virtue of the following:

- He used alcohol to control his emotions.
- He drank alone.
- When he did drink, Jamal sometimes continued to drink until the alcohol let loose his resentment, in the form of anger.
- His conflict with his wife was a direct consequence of his drinking.

If you can identify with Jamal to any significant degree, that insight can be the first step in a solution. Use the steps that follow break out of this cycle.

Step 1: Separate the Past from the Present

For people who are carrying a "bag" of resentments, the first step is to go through that bag and separate the things they feel resentful about into two groups:

- *Resentments from the past.* Jamal had a whole bunch of these, relating to both his father and his mother. Although he'd tried for years not to think about his childhood, when he did, he found that he resented his father deeply because of the emotional and physical abuse he'd inflicted on Jamal throughout his childhood and youth. He also resented his mother. Why? For not standing up for him and, thereby, allowing the abuse to continue. It helped Jamal to share these feelings with a therapist. He experienced some relief just getting that off his chest. He was also able to see how so much of his resentment had its roots in the past.
- *Resentments from the here and now.* Jamal, like all of us, also experienced hurt and angry feelings in response to interactions with others in ordinary life. These were not daily experiences by any means, but they did happen now and then. Spouses, friends, co-workers, and others may not intend to hurt us, yet sometimes they do. Like many survivors of abuse, Jamal was a bit more sensitive in this regard. When his therapist asked Jamal if the term "thin-skinned" accurately described him, Jamal had to admit that it did. For example, even minor remarks that were

not meant to be critical would bother him. Similarly, he was very sensitive to even innocent teasing and did not find it amusing at all.

Step 2: Let Go of the Past

Resentments that have their roots in the past—especially the distant past—are essentially irreconcilable. That leaves us with a choice to make: either to hold on to the resentment that resulted from a past emotional wound or to let it go and move on. Many people have trouble letting go of deep and long-standing resentments, feeling that they have been done an injustice that should be righted. In a sense, they are correct. What they often fail to recognize, however, is that carrying around resentments actually colors your outlook on life. It can deprive you, for instance, of feelings of joy. It is also likely to make you thin-skinned, as Jamal was.

A psychologically healthier choice is to recognize that resentments rooted in the past, though justified, are not worth carrying around. While as children we may have had no choice but to endure abuse and emotional wounds, as adults we do have options. We may have felt forced to suppress emotions like anger and hurt when we were children, but as adults we need not be so constrained.

Jamal was able to let go of his bag of resentments when he shared them with his therapist, who agreed that Jamal's father had been cruel and that Jamal's mother had not intervened to help him. That act of sharing with someone else can also help you, if you are one of those people who are carrying a heavy bag of resentments from the past. Letting go can free you to move on to step 3, the most important part of the change process.

Step 3: Find Your Voice in the Present

Jamal had become so adept at suppressing his feelings as a child that by the time he became an adult, he no longer knew how to give a voice to them. For one thing, he was still saddled with the anxiety he associated with speaking up—with saying even simple things like "That hurt my feelings" or "I'm mad!" Expressing such feelings to his father was dangerous, so Jamal had learned early on to keep them to himself.

A second by-product of his upbringing was that Jamal had never had much practice expressing his feelings. In one of his counseling sessions, Jamal mentioned that it was bothering him that his eight-year-old daughter was giving him an "attitude" whenever he'd correct or direct her. "If I ask her something as simple as 'Can you please clear your plate from the table?' she rolls her eyes and gives me a look," he explained. "I know it isn't that big of a deal, and I know I'm too sensitive, but it still bothers me."

The therapist, who understood Jamal's issue with expressing himself as well as the connection between that and his almost alcoholic drinking, said he did not think this was too small an issue to address. Jamal's daughter was being disrespectful, he explained, and perhaps it would be better for Jamal to address the issue now, before it got worse.

Jamal did not have much experience confronting such situations and expressing his feelings appropriately. In the past, he would have either stuffed his feelings (and built up resentment toward his daughter) or directed his anger inappropriately toward his wife after drinking too much. He might, for example, have accused her of not being enough of a disciplinarian or of allowing the children to take advantage of him. In doing so, he would indirectly be asking his wife to do what his own mother had never done: stick up for him.

Jamal's therapist role played with him how he could appropriately confront his daughter the next time she was disrespectful to Jamal. They both knew this behavior would occur again, and they practiced a few different scenarios. Jamal did not find this easy, and he struggled to choose the right words and the right tone of voice even in these imaginary situations.

In the end, it was the dirty dish that provided Jamal with his opportunity. It was on a Sunday at dinner—a meal that Jamal himself had prepared for everyone. Having finished her meal, his daughter got up to leave the table. Jamal, per the script he'd practiced, spoke up. "Victoria," he said, "please pick up your dishes from the table and put them in the dishwasher."

As expected, the girl rolled her eyes and groaned. But this time, instead of keeping quiet, Jamal spoke up. "Victoria," he said in a firm but controlled voice, "Come here." The girl, surprised to hear her father speak so directly and firmly, stopped in her tracks and looked at him. He, in turn, looked at her. "Every time I ask you to do a simple, common courtesy task like clear your plate at the table, you have that same reaction—you roll your eyes and groan. That hurts my feelings and also makes me mad. You know, we are a family and everyone has to pitch in. That includes little things like clearing the table."

At that point, Jamal's wife—who had no idea that her husband had been working on this issue—took notice of this interaction and piped up. "I agree with your father, Victoria," she said. "I've noticed that too. I don't think you'd like it if your father or I reacted to you that way when you asked something of us. I think you should say you're sorry and work on being more courteous in the future."

This may seem like a small victory, but all things considered it was not. It marked a turning point for Jamal and proved to be an important part of his solution for moving out of the almost alcoholic zone. The more he was able to find his voice and use it effectively, the less need he would have to turn to drinking to anesthetize his emotions.

Keeping Stress at Bay

Most people today lead more stressful lives than many earlier generations did. Despite all of the advantages we enjoy with respect to things like electronics and a growing capacity to treat once-fatal illnesses, life is not easy. The vast majority of families must rely on the incomes from two full-time jobs to make ends meet; today there are many single-parent homes as well. These circumstances create lifestyles that are crammed and complicated. The average American works longer hours than his or her grandparents did, but the resulting wages of today in real buying-power terms have remained stagnant for forty years or more. It is little wonder that people are tempted to turn to alcohol or other drugs to help them cope with the stress they must bear on a daily basis. Little wonder, also, that nerves can become frayed and tempers get short under such circumstances.

Another useful strategy for people who can identify with this scenario is to practice techniques that have been proven to reduce stress and anxiety. Using such techniques allows you to think more clearly, to potentially identify issues that may be bothering you, and to contemplate how you might address them appropriately (instead of using alcohol to avoid them and then potentially exploding).

One such technique is called *mindfulness-based stress reduction*, which was developed to help people cope with chronic pain using minimal or no medication.[25] Although necessary in some cases, pain medications are best used on an acute, time-limited basis. Used long-term, these medications can lose their effectiveness; moreover, many are addicting. As an adjunct to this approach, researchers experimented with a variety of alternative treatments. The method described here—mindfulness meditation—has been found to be effective in reducing pain as well as stress levels. To the extent that chronic stress often motivates people to drink, finding an effective way to reduce stress can be a very helpful part of your solution. When practiced regularly, mindfulness meditation has even been found to lead to increases in "gray matter" in the area of the brain associated with learning, memory, and emotional control.[26] Altogether, these are not bad outcomes for the almost alcoholic seeking a solution!

Mindfulness meditation is best practiced once a day for twenty to thirty minutes in a quiet and comfortable location.[27] Here is what to do:

- Make sure the clothes you are wearing are comfortable and that the room you are in is comfortable as well—no glaring lights or loud background noises.
- Try to make sure you will not be interrupted for at least twenty minutes.
- Set a timer (preferably one with a gentle ring) for half an hour.

- Find a comfortable place to lie down flat—on your back if possible. You may also sit in a chair or on a cushion in a position that allows you to keep your spine straight and your head and neck aligned with your spine without strain.
- Close your eyes and focus your attention on your own breathing. Feel the air go in and then out of your lungs. Breathe naturally—don't try to increase or decrease the rate at which you breathe.
- Allow any outside noises to just pass over you while keeping your attention on your breathing; breathe in and out fully and naturally from your diaphragm, following each of your incoming and outgoing breaths.
- Allow any thoughts you may have to pass in and then out of your mind. Do not get stuck on any one thought—just let the thoughts flow in and out of your consciousness with each breath.
- Allow any other body sensations, including pain, to also flow in and out of your body. Do not focus on pain; rather, let it pass over, through, and out of you like a gentle wave.

Practicing the above daily will have a cumulative effect on your stress level—the longer you practice mindfulness meditation, the less overall stress you will feel. And when you feel less stress, you may feel less of a need to drink in order to relax. Secondly, people who practice mindfulness meditation report that, over time, they are able to think more clearly and calmly. This can be a big advantage if you are trying to deal with issues such as those that Jamal faced. In contrast, a stressed mind does not think clearly. A stressed individual is likely to have trouble thinking of alternative ways of dealing with a problem or deciding the best way to approach it. Finally, a calm mind is the best place to "role play" how you will deal with problematic situations in the future.

• • •

This chapter and the solutions it offers address a common set of emotions—anger and resentment—that almost alcoholics often must learn to deal with. In a culture like ours that tends to normalize drinking, even normalizing the use of alcohol to influence our emotional state—having a cocktail or two to "unwind"—it can be easy to cross the border from normal social drinking into the almost alcoholic zone. The more we come to rely on drinking to either suppress or unleash an emotion, the more at risk we are for moving deeper into the zone. As Jamal's experience attests, that strategy will only worsen our problems. Like Jamal, we need to find and use effective methods of dealing with difficult emotions such as anger and resentment.

11

Overcoming Shame and Guilt

Shame and guilt are among the most powerful and universal of human emotions. When we talk about these two related but distinct terms, we'll use the now commonly accepted definitions: Guilt is feeling bad about something you've done; shame is feeling bad about who you are. Both of these emotions can be the source of intense psychic pain and can easily lead to destructive self-hatred. To make matters worse, we may go to great lengths to conceal feelings of guilt or shame. The result is that individuals who are burdened with guilt or shame carry their secret around, day in and day out, even as it eats away at their self-esteem. We have found a connection exists between shame and drinking, or guilt and drinking, for some almost alcoholics. For members of this group, overcoming self-hatred is a central part of their solution. Let's look at an example.

Shame and Drinking: Maria's Story

Maria was one of six children born to a middle-class family in the Midwest. The family lived a modest but secure lifestyle, although raising six children did keep Maria's mother quite busy. Her father, meanwhile, supplemented his income as an insurance salesman by helping a friend who was a carpenter with side jobs a couple of evenings a week.

Although she was a good student with a talent for art and music that was evident from an early age, the adult Maria told her therapist that she recalled feeling inadequate on some level for as long as she could remember. "I just felt inferior to my brothers and sisters," she explained. "For some reason, I thought they were all more attractive and smarter than I was. It didn't help, I think, that I was the shortest one of my siblings, and for several of my preteen years I held on to my baby fat. No matter how I looked at myself, I felt I just didn't measure up."

In short, Maria felt shame about herself, about who she was as a person. And while she didn't appear to be someone who might have a reason for feeling shame, at that time there was no way Maria could be convinced of that. And it would be difficult to guess that Maria was burdened with shame, as she did not use that word to describe her attitude toward herself, nor did she share her private thoughts about how she didn't "measure up."

Maria said that she'd slimmed down by the time she hit high school, but by then the internal demons that haunted her had already firmly taken root. She expressed it this way: "I felt totally empty inside. I hated myself, and I thought that God must hate me too."

Maria missed quite a few days of school her senior year due to frequent debilitating headaches. By then she had few friends and no best friend; she led a fairly isolated lifestyle. After a neurologist ruled out a physical cause for the headaches, her parents took Maria to see a psychiatrist, who prescribed tranquilizers, thinking anxiety was driving the stress.

Maria was bright enough to keep up with her classes despite missing so much school, and so she was able to graduate with her classmates. She did not, however, graduate near the top of her class, as each of her older siblings had done. That only reinforced the shame she'd been carrying for years.

It was during her senior year in high school that Maria first began to drink. She began by stealing small amounts of brandy and bourbon from her parents' liquor cabinet, and to her pleasant surprise she found that a nip or two did help her to relax. "I discovered that alcohol could somehow make my self-hatred and emptiness go away, at least for a while," she explained.

By the time she was thirty, Maria's drinking had progressed and she was well into the almost alcoholic zone. However, she'd been successful in her life academically, having pulled herself together enough to earn a college degree and then a graduate degree in social work. Her work centered around adolescents, mostly teen girls who, like Maria, were struggling with their self-image. The irony, she explained, was that it took her a long time to make that connection. "As obvious as it seems looking back, I really didn't realize that I was helping teens who suffered from exactly what I suffered from," she told her therapist.

Maria entered therapy not because of her drinking but because she continued to experience periodic bouts of depression that medication had never been able to quell. She also had recently broken off a three-year relationship (actually, he had broken it off), which left her feeling that old emptiness and self-hatred again. She was also feeling hopeless about her prospects for ever finding lasting happiness.

With her therapist, Maria spent time exploring in depth the feelings she'd had, beginning from a very young age, about being somehow inferior—"nothing special" in her words. Although she attended family gatherings, she hated them. "I always put on a happy face," she said, "and pretend that everything is just fine. No one knows I'm dying inside." She was the only one of her siblings who was not yet either married or engaged. The two who were married already had children. She adored her two nieces, but also felt deeply unhappy after she'd visit with them. "It seemed like an impossible dream for me," she said, "that I would ever have a family of my own."

Drinking was the one reliable way that Maria had found for getting relief from these nagging feelings. Though not yet dependent on alcohol, she admitted that she and alcohol definitely had a "relationship," and a serious one at that. "It's the one friend I can count on to make the emptiness go away," she told her therapist. And when the therapist asked Maria if she felt self-hatred, Maria nodded. She also agreed that, as much of a friend as alcohol may have become, relying on it so much was not a formula for future happiness. In fact, her drinking had been a source of conflict in her relationship that had recently ended. In addition, as a trained social worker, Maria was smart enough to know that drinking every day, as she did, probably only worsened her bouts of depression.

Radical Acceptance

When her therapist suggested that Maria's solution begin with a period of abstinence, she agreed. At the same time, she admitted she feared that not drinking would "unleash my demons." The therapist empathized with that and suggested that while

Maria was abstaining from alcohol, they could pursue several of the solutions offered in this book, beginning with some personal reassessment. It was in that context that a somewhat different solution—what psychologist Marsha Linehan has referred to as *radical acceptance*—emerged.[28]

Radical acceptance is akin to the idea of an epiphany that we discussed earlier. The difference is that when we speak of an epiphany, we're typically referring to an experience that alters what people see as their purpose in life. In contrast, radical acceptance begins with an experience that leads someone to suddenly let go of self-hatred—whether based in shame or guilt—and instead to accept who they are at a deep level. The self-hatred that haunted Maria stemmed from self-criticism and a profound feeling of never being good enough. It often also involved an excessive focus on personal faults and flaws (which we all have) to the exclusion of personal assets and positive qualities. This described Maria to a T—and it may also describe you or someone you love.

For Maria, the first step out of self-hatred came in a way that mirrors many epiphanies. A devout Christian, Maria was still in the practice of praying daily (even though she continued to doubt that God loved her). One night, after she'd not had a drink in nearly four weeks and following a discussion with her therapist about the issue underlying Maria's focus on her faults and flaws, she had the following experience: "All at once, the room around me seemed to glow in a golden light. My whole body shivered. Then suddenly a single thought flooded my mind: 'I love myself!'"

That experience marked a turning point in Maria's movement away from almost alcoholism (or worse). It was, she said, as if she were momentarily standing outside of herself and seeing herself as she really was—intelligent, attractive, and successful—for the first time. And that new self-image stuck with her.

Today, three years later, Maria is a rare social drinker. As she describes it, she will enjoy a glass of wine at family gatherings but no more than one. She does not experience any urges to drink more often than that. For the past year, she has been in a new relationship with a man whom she loves and who she believes loves her. They've discussed their shared vision of a family life.

As powerful as it was, Maria's realization that she loved herself actually set off a whole *process* of self-assessment, one that she continues to this day, and one that we offer here as part of the solution for people who can identify with Maria's story.

Guilt and Drinking: Lee's Story

Lee, thirty-eight, had been carrying around a burden of guilt for twenty years.

The guilt stemmed from an experience that had occurred when he was eighteen. It was the summer after his senior year when Lee had gotten his then-girlfriend pregnant. Lee had been accepted to college and was planning to head off to begin the next chapter of his life. His girlfriend, who was a year his junior and who had no plans to go to college after high school, did not want to abort the pregnancy. They talked for hours about the situation. Lee did not press her to have an abortion, yet he was able to say that he did not want to give up college.

The next day when they met again, Lee's girlfriend told him she was going forward with the pregnancy. She then told

Lee that she would agree to keep his parenthood secret in exchange for his promise to permanently and totally exit her (and the baby's) life. He agreed, and she kept her word, despite enduring heavy criticism from her family and being ostracized at school.

For his part, Lee went off to college, where he studied hard and did well. From there he went on to law school and eventually to a corporate position where he specialized in tax law. As he explained it, "My job is to help the company pay as few taxes as possible—preferably none at all."

Lee returned home only rarely after leaving for college. In the summers, he made a point of using his college connections to find work in other areas of the country. The reason he gave his parents, which they reluctantly accepted, was that this was a chance for him to see other places and get a sense of where he might want to eventually settle down.

Lee had been married for five years and had a three-year-old son when he decided to seek counseling ostensibly for a lingering depression. Despite his financial success, he said, "I just don't feel happy a lot of the time." This general feeling of unhappiness had troubled him on and off for years, but it had become noticeably more intense since his son had been born. Over this same period, Lee's drinking had steadily increased. He'd always enjoyed a cocktail after work, but at the time of his first counseling session he was up to three a night—and often more on weekends. He'd gained weight, and his wife had expressed concern about both his drinking and his depressed, irritable mood.

As you might guess, Lee was carrying around a burden of guilt and had been doing so for a long time. Although it wasn't always in the forefront of his mind, on some level it was always there—the feeling that he had "abandoned" his first child. After his son was born, Lee sometimes had nightmares. In some of these nightmares he was in a shopping mall and could not find his son. In others—and these were the worst—he was making arrangements to give his son away. In either case, he would wake up with a start and in a depressed mood that lingered all day. He'd never told his wife or anyone else about these dreams, nor had he ever disclosed what he'd done at age eighteen.

Lee's drinking was clearly driven by his guilt. Like Maria, Lee had a turning point, but his came in a therapist's office. It happened after Lee—again like Maria—had taken his therapist's advice to stop drinking for a while. And it happened when Lee, looking visibly agitated, began a session by saying, "I have something I want to talk about today. I've never talked to anyone about this, but I really think I need to now." And with that statement, Lee opened the door to healing his guilt and self-hatred.

Lee and his therapist talked for many hours and over many weeks about the pregnancy and the decisions it led him and his former girlfriend to make. In time, he came to see that each of them was doing what, at age eighteen and seventeen, they thought was best. The girlfriend wanted to keep the baby, and she was prepared to set Lee free. Indeed, she seemed to want it that way. And though he had every right to feel sad that he had never seen this child (he'd learned through the grapevine that it was a boy), he did not really deserve to bear the burden of guilt for a decision that he did not make alone, but mutually. Lee did not, in other words, "abandon" a child so much as he and his girlfriend had opted to go their separate ways. It was natural to feel guilt about committing a specific act that went against his values, but it was unnatural to translate that guilt into self-hatred and carry those feelings into the rest of his life. In time, and with the support of his therapist, Lee made some progress into expressing his remorse, forgiving himself, and letting go of his guilt—and with it, his long-standing self-hatred. He, too, was able to discover the healing power of radical acceptance.

Pursuing Radical Acceptance

It is possible to facilitate radical acceptance. The key is to engage in an ongoing process of honest self-assessment in combination with an ongoing assessment of others. The reciprocal nature of this process is critical, for without it the almost alcoholic who is burdened with self-hatred is likely to overstate personal flaws while understating those of others. Conversely, the almost alcoholic will likely minimize his or her personal virtues while exaggerating those of others. That's exactly what Maria did. Viewed through her eyes, her siblings were virtuous whereas she was riddled with flaws. Her epiphany-like experience enabled her to correct that imbalance and opened the door, for the first time in her life, to self-acceptance: to liking herself for who she was.

To pursue radical self-acceptance in your own life, review the following chart and then create your own chart in your journal. You will need to complete the checklists in the chart for *yourself* and also for *two significant people in your life.* This exercise will only help you achieve or maintain self-acceptance if you take this balanced approach.

The Character Inventory chart is divided in two checklists: *Assets* and *Flaws.* Each of us has a character that is composed of a mixture of both assets and flaws, although the *degree* to which we have such assets and flaws can vary. One person, for example, can suffer from jealousy to a great extent, whereas someone else may experience only a milder form of jealousy. Accordingly, for each asset or flaw you identify, rate it either 1 (somewhat), 2 (moderately), or 3 (extremely) as it describes you or either of the two loved ones you include in your chart. You can, of course, add other flaws and assets to the chart and you can create more than one chart, comparing yourself to more significant others in your life—we encourage you to do so.

Lastly, the character inventories you will create using this chart must be balanced. That is, *the number of flaws you identify must equal the number of assets, for yourself and for the others listed in your chart.*

Live and Let Live

One of the popular slogans in Twelve Step recovery groups is "Live and let live." Basically, this is a statement of self-acceptance and acceptance of others. An *inability* to accept one's self—the good and the bad, the assets and the flaws—is an ongoing invitation to use alcohol to anesthetize that inner unhappiness.

If you incorporate this exercise into your solution, it will be important to make it a living document and not just something you do once and file away. Changing an established self-image is not an easy task, and it would be a mistake to assume that anyone can do it in a single sitting. Maria certainly couldn't; rather, her epiphany-like experience marked the beginning, not

Character Inventory

Yourself		Significant Other 1: ______		Significant Other 2: ______	
ASSETS		**ASSETS**		**ASSETS**	
Generous	1 2 3	Generous	1 2 3	Generous	1 2 3
Kind	1 2 3	Kind	1 2 3	Kind	1 2 3
Loving	1 2 3	Loving	1 2 3	Loving	1 2 3
Helpful	1 2 3	Helpful	1 2 3	Helpful	1 2 3
Humble	1 2 3	Humble	1 2 3	Humble	1 2 3
Compassionate	1 2 3	Compassionate	1 2 3	Compassionate	1 2 3
Trustworthy	1 2 3	Trustworthy	1 2 3	Trustworthy	1 2 3
Brave	1 2 3	Brave	1 2 3	Brave	1 2 3
FLAWS		**FLAWS**		**FLAWS**	
Selfish	1 2 3	Selfish	1 2 3	Selfish	1 2 3
Stingy	1 2 3	Stingy	1 2 3	Stingy	1 2 3
Jealous	1 2 3	Jealous	1 2 3	Jealous	1 2 3
Arrogant	1 2 3	Arrogant	1 2 3	Arrogant	1 2 3
Exploitive	1 2 3	Exploitive	1 2 3	Exploitive	1 2 3
Self-pitying	1 2 3	Self-pitying	1 2 3	Self-pitying	1 2 3
Mean	1 2 3	Mean	1 2 3	Mean	1 2 3
Careless	1 2 3	Careless	1 2 3	Careless	1 2 3

the end, of a change process. Beginnings, however, are important, and when people change how they fundamentally feel about themselves, they're creating a vital tool to use in their journey out of the almost alcoholic zone.

Radical acceptance means learning to accept and like yourself for who you are. It also means not exaggerating your own flaws—or minimizing your character assets—in comparison to those of others, as Maria, Lee, and so many people who carry the emotional burdens of shame and guilt are inclined to do. And while radical acceptance begins inside of us, it can be immensely helpful to find the courage, first, to share your old and distorted self-image with someone you trust and, second, to talk with that person about an alternative self-assessment based on this exercise. For Maria, that was her therapist. We've known others who have turned to clergy, family members, and trusted friends for this, often with equally good results.

• • •

So far our solutions have rested on proven techniques for changing things ranging from simple behaviors (refusal skills) to emotions (resentment) to one's basic sense of identity and self-image. All of these can become ongoing parts of a solution for the almost alcoholic. In the next chapter, we shift gears and examine some different kinds of solutions, including medication.

12

When Self-Help Isn't Enough: Other Drugs and Other Disorders

Most people who realize that they are almost alcoholics and make a decision to change will be able to successfully alter their drinking patterns and make a change for the positive by using some or all of the solutions presented in this book. Occasionally, though, some almost alcoholics will continue to encounter problems controlling their alcohol consumption despite their best efforts. There can be many different reasons for this, including a mental illness that may contribute to almost alcoholic drinking. In other cases, a person's drinking may have gotten deep into the almost alcoholic zone, or they may have left the almost alcoholic zone altogether and crossed over into alcoholism, from which it's impossible to return to normal social drinking. In these cases, either a medical intervention or the assistance of an addiction professional is recommended.

How Far In Are You?

If an almost alcoholic encounters difficulty in changing a harmful drinking pattern, several possibilities must be considered. First, has drinking advanced to the point of dependence? Consider the following example.

Grace's Story

Grace's daughter, Kerry, recounted her family's concern about her mother when she seemed to be experiencing early symptoms of Alzheimer's disease. However, Grace's subsequent specialty consultation with a neurologist, along with testing for dementia, did not reveal the typical features of Alzheimer's disease. No one in the family had ever suspected that alcohol could be playing a role in the symptoms the family saw. After all, this woman was an ordained minister—indeed, she was the pastor of her church.

The clue that led to the correct diagnosis was found as a result of a routine blood test. Chronic, heavy drinking can deplete two important B vitamins: thiamine and folic acid. Deficiency of these B vitamins can lead to neurological and cognitive changes. Lack of folic acid causes red blood cells to become too big, and this finding tipped off the clinician to the possibility of an alcohol-related problem, which turned out to be the case.

Interestingly, 5 percent of alcoholics have central nervous system problems, but about 80 percent of these cases go undiagnosed.[29] In the case of Kerry's mother, a simple lab test raised enough suspicion to justify asking this upstanding woman about her drinking. As it turned out, Grace was indeed an alcoholic, and a fairly advanced one at that.

Grace's drinking had increased following the loss of her husband to cancer ten years earlier. Although able to maintain outward appearances and continue functioning as a pastor, she had taken to drinking fairly large quantities of flavored brandies and schnapps daily. She did this as she worked on her weekly sermons in the day, after visiting a sick parishioner, and on into the evening. In public or visiting with family, she never drank in excess, and no one suspected she was drinking on the sly. Without that blood test's tipoff to her primary care physician, she might have continued this pattern of drinking indefinitely. She could even have been prescribed an expensive Alzheimer's drug that would have been ineffective in solving her problem instead of the inexpensive vitamin therapy that was really needed. Of course, Grace also needed to address her alcoholism—the root of the problem.

Grace's story is a case of classic alcohol dependence. We include it here to make a point, which is that sometimes a true alcoholic might appear (or want to appear) to be an almost alcoholic. In the end, a person's honesty about his or her drinking may be the only definitive test to prevent unnecessary and possibly risky medical interventions.

Other Drugs

In Grace's case, malnutrition, as revealed through her blood work, hinted at a drinking problem. In other cases, drinking problems might be a manifestation of another condition. Since most almost alcoholics are able to make changes in their drinking behaviors, those who struggle should wonder whether something else might be contributing to their drinking. For example, approximately 43 percent of people who are alcohol dependent in the United States have another drug use disorder.[30] This means that an almost alcoholic must be willing to face this possibility and address any problems with both alcohol and the other drugs. For example, curtailing alcohol use while increasing marijuana use will not solve any problems. On the other hand, not drinking while maintaining or even reducing marijuana use is a first step in the right direction. For the almost alcoholic man or woman, the ultimate goal will be abstinence from illicit drugs and either abstinence from alcohol or a return to normal social drinking. For the person who is dependent on one or more drugs, including alcohol, abstinence supported by a program of recovery is the answer.

Co-occurring Conditions

A significant number of men and women must simultaneously face drinking use disorders, including almost alcoholic drinking, *and* a mental illness. Professionals call these "co-occurring" conditions or disorders, and both require treatment *at the same time*. Whereas it once was thought, for example, that a drinking problem would simply "disappear" if a mental illness was treated—or that each disorder needed to be treated separately at different times and places—we now know this is not true.

Untreated psychiatric conditions *can* hinder an almost alcoholic in his or her efforts at stopping or reducing drinking. One large study showed that 47 percent of people who were alcohol dependent had an anxiety disorder, while 41 percent had a mood disorder. About 32 percent of patients who were alcohol dependent exhibited conduct disorder symptoms and 13 percent showed symptoms of personality disorder.[31] Which came first: the depression or anxiety, or the drinking problem?

Although some people become stuck on this chicken-or-egg question, a better way of thinking about the issue is to consider the chicken *and* the egg. In other words, anxiety or depression might have contributed to the development of problem drinking, but addressing the psychiatric disorder and the drinking issues simultaneously makes the most sense.

Often adequately treating an anxiety disorder or depression can help with an alcohol problem as well, because the almost alcoholic may have been "self-medicating"—trying to contain his or her emotional distress through drinking. Remember that drinking to influence your emotions is one of the signs of being an almost alcoholic. Instead of self-medicating with alcohol, psychotherapy in combination with medications can effectively treat these conditions.

Other disorders, including sleep disorders, attention deficit hyperactivity disorder (ADHD), personality disorders, and subtle forms of psychosis, can also be present at times and represent added challenges for the almost alcoholic who is seeking a solution. There are several medications that, along with behavioral modification techniques, have been proven to help people with sleep disorders and ADHD. Certain forms of psychotherapy (sometimes in combination with medication) can also help people with personality or other more severe disorders, such as one in which a person has trouble with behavior control and is troubled by frequent thoughts of suicide.

Together Is Better

Although most almost alcoholics do not have a serious co-occurring psychiatric disorder, such as schizophrenia or bipolar disorder, a substantial number do suffer with one or even more milder and treatable psychiatric conditions, such as depression and anxiety. A double-barreled approach that treats the hazardous alcohol use while also aggressively addressing the co-occurring psychiatric condition usually hits the target. This means that people who are almost alcoholic and who are having trouble cutting back or stopping their alcohol use—even as they use the solutions presented here—might benefit from a thorough evaluation by a mental health professional who can diagnose and treat the psychiatric conditions that can contribute to continued almost alcoholic drinking.

The person with psychiatric *and* alcohol problems is best served by adequately and appropriately treating both at the same time.

Does alcohol take the edge off your anxiety? Does a drink or two diminish the depressed way you have been feeling the past month? Does a six-pack of beer help you forget about all the problems your attention deficit symptoms caused that day? We've addressed the issue of emotions and drinking, and how one can lead to the other. However, if the solutions we've presented so far don't seem to be working for you despite an honest effort, you may want to consider whether you might have co-occurring conditions. You may be almost alcoholic, but your problems may also be related to common conditions such as anxiety, depression, ADHD, or a sleep disorder. Often people who do have an underlying psychiatric disorder do not realize this. Or if they do suspect it, they don't act on it. Usually the reason for their hesitation is a fear of being stigmatized as "mentally ill." Indeed, there was a time when people who suffered from depression or anxiety could find themselves stigmatized. But we have come a long way from that. We've come so far, in fact, that it's difficult to watch television or read a magazine without being exposed to an ad for one kind of psychiatric medication or another. So rather than trying to ignore this possibility or continuing to self-medicate your emotional distress—which will not make it go away—we suggest you look into an approach that helps with both problems at once. That means, potentially, using the solutions presented here *in combination with* medical treatment.

Getting help for co-occurring conditions involves a simple two-step process. The first step is to consult with a professional who has training and experience in diagnosing and treating *both* psychiatric disorders *and* drinking problems. This may be a psychiatrist, clinical psychologist, or an appropriately trained social worker, family therapist, or addictions counselor. If, indeed, the conclusion you come to in collaboration with this professional is that you do have not one but two problems to deal with, you need to consider your options. Treatment for both of these conditions involves adding some professional help to what you are doing for yourself.

Most of the time the second step starts with psychotherapy, especially if what you are faced with is a milder form of a psychiatric illness. Some sleep disorders, as well as certain forms of depression and anxiety disorders, respond quite well to cognitive-behavioral forms of psychotherapy, which involve learning more positive forms of self-talk to replace the negative messages that perpetuate these conditions. A recently widowed woman, for instance, would benefit far more from supportive psychotherapy than the scotch and soda she uses to fill the void since her husband died.

Medications

Sometimes a medication, when added to talk therapy, provides a better outcome than either treatment alone. After all, psychiatric conditions such as depression, anxiety disorders, and ADHD have a biological basis. Indeed, research has consistently shown clear imbalances in the brain chemistry of people with these diagnoses. Medications can restore balance in their brain chemistry, thereby lessening—if not eliminating—many of their symptoms. Some of the medications frequently prescribed for the most common psychiatric disorders are discussed in appendix A.

Let's say an almost alcoholic takes our advice, consults with a mental health professional, and learns that he or she has a "clean psychiatric bill of health." Does this mean that medication should not be prescribed? As in other things in life, "for every rule, exceptions exist." Although the overwhelming majority of almost alcoholics will not need medications approved for the treatment of alcohol abuse or dependence, a few might. In rare instances, an almost alcoholic might continue to struggle with changing his or her drinking behavior despite trying our solutions *and* psychotherapy. In these rare cases, a clinician might suggest that a medication approved for alcohol abuse or dependence be prescribed. In appendix B, we discuss the use of "off-label" medications (medications developed for disorders other than the one for which they are prescribed) and those developed specifically to reduce craving in alcoholics and other addicts.

• • •

Although the medications developed for mood disorders do not reduce cravings for alcohol very much, they do effectively treat depression and anxiety. These medications and others often improve the quality of life for people with psychiatric conditions and this can translate into a healthier relationship with alcohol for someone who is almost alcoholic. Unfortunately, most of the research and medical literature thus far has focused on alcohol dependence and contains very little information about using medications to help people who are almost alcoholics. Almost alcoholic is a new concept, but we hope that clinical researchers will recognize that almost alcoholics also struggle in significant ways even though they fall outside the current diagnostic "net." Research is a time-consuming and costly endeavor, but we feel that any investment in understanding and treating the almost alcoholic will pay big dividends.

13

Is Abstinence the Better Choice?

Here in part 2, we have presented a range of solutions that people who are almost alcoholic can turn to if their goal is to move away from the almost alcoholic drinking zone and back toward normal social drinking. We have seen many people use these solutions with success. The vast majority of these individuals have crossed the line into the almost alcoholic zone without consciously realizing it. Many of them have not ventured so far across that they experience physical and/or psychological symptoms of dependency. Most prominent among the symptoms, as we discussed earlier, are these:

- *Withdrawal:* physical symptoms such as sweating, nausea, stomachaches or headaches when a person tries to stop drinking
- *Preoccupation:* thinking about drinking almost all the time and/or becoming irritable when unable to drink, also referred to as *craving*

- *Continuing to drink despite severe negative consequences,* including the following:
  - — *Physical* (diabetes, hypertension, liver disease, etc.)
  - — *Legal* (arrests for driving while intoxicated)
  - — *Financial* (spending excessively on alcohol, making poor financial decisions while under the influence)
  - — *Psychological* (depression)
  - — *Behavioral* (aggressiveness, sexual victimization)
- *Hiding supplies:* "stashing" alcohol in various places so others cannot find it

Symptoms such as those listed can make it impossible for people, despite their best intentions, to return safely to the normal social drinking zone. If even one of these symptoms describes you, we strongly recommend that your solution begin with a ninety-day period of abstinence from drinking.

Decide for Yourself

Many people assume that the fellowship of Alcoholics Anonymous demands that anyone attending its meetings declare that he or she is a full-fledged alcoholic. In reality, however, the only stated "requirement" for attending these meetings is "a desire to stop drinking." We have known many people who have gone to AA for this very purpose, even though they privately were not sure whether they were truly alcoholics, as opposed to almost alcoholics. Interestingly, though, research has firmly established that people who attend AA meetings—whether they are alcoholics or almost alcoholics—have a better chance of staying sober than people who do not.[32] If you find yourself struggling with our ninety-day recommendation, you might want to try a few open AA meetings as a way of getting some additional support. (As the name suggests, open meetings are open to anyone, whereas closed meetings are for people who are there specifically to recover from alcoholism.) Keep in mind that you do not have to make a long-term commitment to AA to make use of its support—you don't even have to state that you are an alcoholic.

In addition to AA, other support groups have a common goal of helping men and women who want to abstain from drinking. These include Secular Organizations for Sobriety (SOS) and Women for Sobriety (WFS) among others. These aren't as prevalent as AA meetings, but they are usually available in larger metropolitan areas. The best way to find out if these support groups are available in your area is to do an Internet search. We are supportive of all of these mutual support groups that seek to help people stay sober. If AA has any advantage in this regard, it is that it is widespread. You can find AA meetings in virtually any community by visiting www.AA.org. In most communities, a diversity of meetings (for men, for women, and so on) will also be listed.

Bill Wilson, the cofounder of AA, avoided trying to convince anyone that he or she was an alcoholic. Instead, he put it this way:

> We do not like to pronounce any individual as alcoholic, but you can quickly diagnose yourself. Step into the nearest bar and try some controlled drinking. Try to drink and stop abruptly. Try it more than once. It will not take long for you to decide, if you are honest with yourself about it.[33]

His advice sounds reasonable to us as well—as long as you don't plan on driving after you've taken one of these "tests"!

Here's another tool to help you decide whether you would be wise to begin your solution with a minimum ninety-day period of abstinence. Go through the following inventory and, in your journal, list all of the items that apply to you:

Ways I Have Tried to Control or Limit My Drinking

____ Counting how many drinks I've had and trying to set a limit

____ Measuring my drinks

____ Drinking from a smaller glass

____ Never drinking before a certain hour

____ Drinking only at home

____ Drinking only outside my home

____ Drinking only expensive wine (beer or liquor)

____ Buying small (not large) bottles of wine (beer or liquor)

____ Drinking only cocktails

____ Drinking only wine (or beer) instead of hard liquor

____ Trying not to drink alone

____ Trying not to drink at parties

____ Making a promise to myself to stop if I ever got drunk again

____ Taking medication to see if that would decrease my desire to drink

Now, think about your responses again and determine how many of these methods that you've tried *have not worked in the long run.* If you can identify with several of the ways that have not worked for you, you are more likely to have success in using the various solutions offered here in part 2 if you begin with a ninety-day break from all drinking.

Whether you will eventually be able to return to normal social drinking depends in part on how diligent you are in pursuing the solutions we offer. It also depends on just how far you have ventured into the almost alcoholic zone. That zone, as we have pointed out, is quite large, but someone in this zone can eventually cross into true alcoholism. If that happens, then we suggest using all of our solutions not as a way of returning to normal social drinking, but as a formula for staying sober. And if that isn't enough, we strongly recommend seeking professional help and/or, at the very least, giving AA a fair shot. Here's what we mean by giving AA a fair shot:

- Go to meetings consistently (at least three per week at first—or every day for ninety days if you feel especially vulnerable).
- Go to several different meetings until you find one that you can commit to as your "home group."
- Find a sponsor (someone in AA who has at least two years of solid sobriety and is someone you think can help you stay sober).
- Work through the Twelve Steps of recovery recommended in the AA book *Alcoholics Anonymous* (called the Big Book by members).

A Final Word

We believe that you will have found this book useful if you have approached the issue of drinking with an open mind and if you have done a brave and honest assessment of your own drinking—or have helped a loved one to do so. With that as a starting point, most readers will want to pursue a plan that incorporates as many of our solutions as possible in an effort to leave the almost alcoholic zone and return to normal social drinking. As we said at the outset, there are millions of almost alcoholics, and we believe these solutions will work for them if they apply them with diligence. If that is not enough, an even braver step to take may be to accept that social drinking is no longer a viable option and that our solutions are better applied to staying sober—or that professional help and/or AA is necessary if you've accepted that you're a true alcoholic. For those who have any doubt that a life without drinking can be worthwhile, we suggest simply visiting a few open AA meetings and listening to the stories of personal and spiritual renewal that are shared in those rooms.

We also believe that, like so many of the almost alcoholics we've worked with, you'll find a richer, more rewarding life without using alcohol to medicate or escape your emotional pain. And we hope that, like many of these people, with a mind unclouded by alcohol, you will have your own "epiphany" and awaken to the life you've envisioned, a life that reflects your true values and highest aspirations.

A Note on Our Solutions

The past twenty years have seen a significant increase in research on alcohol abuse and its treatment. This includes many "controlled clinical trials" that can definitively establish the effectiveness of a particular treatment. All of the solutions we have presented in this book are based on what has come to be called "evidence-based treatment," meaning treatments that have been shown to be effective through controlled clinical trials.

Readers who want to learn more about the evidence-based treatments we have relied on can use the notes at the end of the book. Additional recommended resources are the National Registry of Evidence-based Programs and Practices, or NREPP (www.nrepp.samhsa.gov), and the American Psychological Association's listing of Empirically Supported Treatments (www.apa.org).

appendix A

Common Medications for Psychiatric Disorders

Today, several classes of antidepressants are available and some of these antidepressants are also approved to treat various anxiety disorders. This can be good news for the almost alcoholic who is also dealing with anxiety and depression. Several antidepressants in the *selective serotonin reuptake inhibitor* class (SSRI for short) effectively treat both depression and anxiety disorders. Fluoxetine, sertraline, paroxetine, and citalopram are called antidepressants because the US Food and Drug Administration (FDA) approved them to treat depression. Later studies concluded, however, that SSRI medications do a good job treating anxiety disorders as well. Another antidepressant, the slow-release form of bupropion, has approval for smoking cessation as well as depression. Bupropion has relatively few side effects and is often used in persons with bipolar depression due to a lower risk for mania. However, at higher dosages, it can increase the risk of seizures. Persons who binge drink put themselves at higher risk for seizures, so even low dosages of bupropion could increase that risk.

These medications have relatively few side effects compared to older medications, and they now come in generic versions, so the cost should not stand in the way of treatment.

Side effects, on the other hand, occasionally can be used to one's advantage. For instance, an older antidepressant—trazodone—was known for causing drowsiness; therefore, it is often prescribed to address insomnia in some persons with depression, anxiety, and even sleep disorders.

Benzodiazepines, another class of medications, effectively treat anxiety and sleep problems. Drugs in this class include diazepam (Valium), alprazolam (Xanax), and others. Benzodiazepines are used in detoxification centers to prevent dangerous symptoms of alcohol withdrawal, but this is done under careful medical monitoring since these medications can be addictive. For people who struggle with heavy alcohol use, taking a benzodiazepine for anxiety might reduce their drinking, but it could also lead to dependence on the benzodiazepine in place of alcohol.

Moreover, the effects of benzodiazepines are similar to those of alcohol, and these effects will magnify each other. Diazepam is particularly prone to this magnification because it stays active longer than other medications in this class. A person may take diazepam early in the day and assume that drinking that night will be safe. But given the drug's long half-life, the interaction between the residual diazepam and moderate drinking later that evening could result in an unexpectedly high level of intoxication. Suffice it to say that benzodiazepines play an important role in alcohol detoxification, but in most cases this class of drugs should be avoided until alcohol problems are under control to avoid adverse interactions and the possibility of addiction.

Tricyclic antidepressants like amitriptyline can help patients who have sleep problems and poor appetite. Amitriptyline and similar medications can also treat chronic pain more effectively than the transient relief that alcohol provides.

Regardless of what we call them, medications can sometimes help with two or three problems at the same time: depression, anxiety, and almost alcoholic problems.

appendix B

Medications for Alcohol Abuse and Dependence

A clinician has two choices after deciding that a pharmacological intervention is necessary to treat alcohol abuse or dependence: off-label medications, or medications specifically designed to reduce craving.

Off-Label Medications

The term *off-label* refers to using a medication in a manner different from what the FDA approved it for. An off-label use can take various forms. For example, prescribing a drug above the approved or recommended dosage range would be an off-label use. Clinicians sometimes try this after observing some clear benefits of a particular medication in the approved range, but also see that their patient struggles with residual symptoms such as depression, anxiety, or mood swings. The prescribing clinician must then make a judgment call about whether to switch to another medication, add another medication, or

nudge the currently prescribed medication above the approved dosage. Sometimes going beyond the approved dosage range makes the most sense from a side-effect and cost perspective.

The term *off-label* use also applies to using a medication for a condition for which it has not received approval. Once all the approved drugs for a condition have been tried and failed at the recommended dosage ranges, the patient and clinician have little choice but to resort to off-label use of medications. If a medication is used off-label, the prescribing clinician must inform the patient that the medication is being used at a higher dosage or for a different reason than approved. The patient should realize that off-label prescribing may not achieve the desired benefits or might cause unexpected side effects; however, these issues occasionally occur even under the approved conditions.

Drugs That Target Alcohol Use

At present, the FDA has approved three medications to treat alcohol *dependence:* disulfiram, naltrexone, and acamprosate. None of these drugs, however, are approved specifically for the almost alcoholic as defined here. That said, if other approaches do not work, a clinician attuned to the repeated setbacks that an almost alcoholic is having in changing drinking patterns might recommend an off-label use of medication that has been approved to reduce alcohol use or prevent relapse.

Each of these drugs has a different twist on the way it can reduce a person's desire for a martini with a twist. Disulfiram has been around the longest and has a track record dating back to 1947. This medication makes a person appear "allergic" to alcohol. That is, if a person consumes any alcohol while

taking disulfiram, he or she will experience a number of very unpleasant consequences, including heart palpitations, flushing, nausea, vomiting, and headache. These effects should seem familiar, since many of them can also occur whenever a person drinks too much.

Disulfiram blocks an enzyme called acetaldehyde dehydrogenase that processes alcohol in the body. A chemical called acetaldehyde quickly builds up and the person starts to feel sick quite rapidly as a result. Many people of Asian descent have low levels of the acetaldehyde dehydrogenase enzyme, so they tend to have a natural protection against alcohol abuse and dependence. Disulfiram gives a person all the unpleasant effects of heavy drinking and a hangover without any of the pleasant effects associated with alcohol. (We are talking about that humdinger of a hangover feeling that makes a person swear to never touch alcohol again.) In alcohol-dependent persons disulfiram can reduce "drinking days"—how often a person drinks—by as much as 50 percent. On occasion, the alcohol-disulfiram reaction may be severe and medical treatment could be required. Of course, a person could simply stop taking disulfiram, so involving a spouse or significant other could help ensure that the almost alcoholic who decides to try this solution takes the medication regularly.

Naltrexone reduces drinking in a different way. Instead of feeling miserable whenever you drink, as with disulfiram, a person taking naltrexone simply experiences a reduction in the rewarding effects of alcohol. Naltrexone blocks the action of opiates, including the natural ones our brains make. Anyone who has experienced the "runner's high" is familiar with the way that natural endorphins or enkephalins released in the brain can create a mild euphoria. A similar process is thought to happen with alcohol, but naltrexone seems to diminish the rewarding properties of alcohol.

Naltrexone appears to work best in people who have a strong family history of alcohol dependence—in other words, those who seem to be intrinsically vulnerable to developing a tolerance for alcohol that allows them to move quickly and deeply into the almost alcoholic zone. In people who are alcohol dependent, the use of naltrexone has been found to result in a reduction in drinking days. In people who are almost alcoholic, naltrexone theoretically could reduce the rewarding effects of alcohol, thereby helping the individual make positive changes in drinking patterns.

Both disulfiram and naltrexone carry a slight risk for liver problems, so these medications should be avoided in patients with liver disease. Periodic blood tests can be checked to make sure that the liver remains healthy. Even though a long-acting form of naltrexone can be administered as a shot, the expense and hassles of injections might not appeal to an almost alcoholic. The long-acting naltrexone injection remains a reasonable option, however, for someone who is alcohol dependent. If a person has liver disease and decides to drink alcohol despite the potential consequences, that person probably has stepped over the line separating the almost alcoholic from the true alcoholic.

Acamprosate is a medication that can help prevent relapse by moderating the symptoms of prolonged alcohol withdrawal. An almost alcoholic by definition would not experience prolonged withdrawal, so acamprosate offers little help for people who are the focus of this book—unless your conclusion is that you are an alcoholic and need to pursue any and all viable solutions.

All of the medications described require prescriptions and need to be monitored by clinicians licensed to safely prescribe them. Anyone tempted to try one of these medications by taking pills prescribed to a friend or family member should remember the old adage: a physician who has himself as his own physician has a fool for his physician. The stakes can be high: for instance, the tricyclic antidepressants mentioned can be lethal if someone takes the wrong dosage. The proper medication dosage depends on a person's age, size, and underlying medical conditions, as well as other prescription or nonprescription medications he or she may be taking. With this in mind, any person would be wise to seek appropriate medical help rather than foolishly misusing someone else's medication.

appendix C

The Twelve Steps of Alcoholics Anonymous

1. We admitted we were powerless over alcohol—that our lives had become unmanageable.
2. Came to believe that a Power greater than ourselves could restore us to sanity.
3. Made a decision to turn our will and our lives over to the care of God *as we understood Him.*
4. Made a searching and fearless moral inventory of ourselves.
5. Admitted to God, to ourselves, and to another human being the exact nature of our wrongs.
6. Were entirely ready to have God remove all these defects of character.
7. Humbly asked Him to remove our shortcomings.
8. Made a list of all persons we had harmed, and became willing to make amends to them all.
9. Made direct amends to such people wherever possible, except when to do so would injure them or others.
10. Continued to take personal inventory and when we were wrong promptly admitted it.
11. Sought through prayer and meditation to improve our conscious contact with God *as we understood Him,* praying only for knowledge of His will for us and the power to carry that out.
12. Having had a spiritual awakening as the result of these steps, we tried to carry this message to alcoholics, and to practice these principles in all our affairs.

The Twelve Steps of AA are taken from *Alcoholics Anonymous,* 4th ed., published by Alcoholics Anonymous World Services, Inc., New York, NY, 59–60.

notes

1. National Institute on Alcohol Abuse and Alcoholism, "National Epidemiologic Survey on Alcohol and Related Conditions: Related Findings," *Alcohol Research & Health* 29, no. 2 (2006).

2. National Institute on Alcohol Abuse and Alcoholism, "Young Adult Drinking," *Alcohol Alert* 68 (April 2006).

3. American Psychiatric Association, *Diagnostic and Statistical Manual of Mental Disorders*, 4th ed., text rev. (Washington, DC: American Psychiatric Association, 2000).

4. "What Is Alcoholism?" National Institute on Alcohol Abuse and Alcoholism, updated February 2007. http://www.niaaa.nih.gov/FAQs/General-English/Pages/default.aspx.

5. K. Brower and J. Hall, "Effects of Age and Alcoholism on Sleep: A Controlled Study," *Journal of Studies on Alcohol* 62, no. 3 (2001): 335–43.

6. M. Willenbring, "Treatment of Heavy Drinking and Alcohol Use Disorders," in *Principles of Addiction Medicine*, 4th ed., ed. R. Ries (Philadelphia: Lippincott Williams & Wilkins, 2009).

7. National Institute on Alcohol Abuse and Alcoholism, "Alcohol Research: A Lifespan Perspective," *Alcohol Alert* 74 (January 2008).

8. J. Saunders, O. Aasland, T. Babor, J. de la Fuente, and M. Grant, "Development of the Alcohol Use Disorders Identification Test (AUDIT)," *Addiction* 88, no. 6 (June 1993): 791–804; National Institute on Alcohol Abuse and Alcoholism, "Screening for Alcohol Use and Alcohol-Related Problems," *Alcohol Alert* 65 (April 2005).

9. B. Grant, F. Stinson, D. Dawson, S. Chou, M. Dufour, W. Compton, R. Pickering, and K. Kaplan, "Prevalence and Co-Occurrence of Substance Use Disorders and Independent Mood and Anxiety Disorders: Results from the National Epidemiologic Survey on Alcohol and Related Conditions," *Archives of General Psychiatry* 61, no. 8 (August 2004): 807–16.

10. Brower and Hall, "Effects of Age and Alcoholism on Sleep."

11. V. Bagnardi, M. Blangiardo, C. La Vecchia, and G. Corrao, "Alcohol Consumption and the Risk of Cancer: A Meta-analysis," *Alcohol Research & Health* 25 (2001): 263–70.

12. National Institute on Alcohol Abuse and Alcoholism, "Alcohol Metabolism: An Update," *Alcohol Alert* 72 (July 2007).

13. C. Knapp, *Drinking: A Love Story* (New York: Dial Press, 1997).

14. National Institute of Mental Health, "Epidemiologic Catchment Area Study: 1980–1985" (Rockville, MD: US Dept. of Health and Human Services, National Institute of Mental Health, ICPSR Study No. 06153, 1992).

15. Grant et al., "Prevalence and Co-Occurrence of Substance Use Disorders."

16. E. Triffleman, "Gender Differences in a Controlled Pilot Study of Psychosocial Treatments in Substance Dependent Patients with Post-Traumatic Stress Disorder," *Alcoholism Treatment Quarterly* 18 (November 2000): 113–26.

17. "University of Rhode Island Change Assessment Scale: URICA," HABITS Lab, Psychology Department, University of Maryland, Baltimore County. http://www.umbc.edu/psyc/habits/content/ttm_measures/urica/index.html.

18. J. Nowinski, *Six Questions That Can Change Your Life* (New York: Rodale, 2002).

19. Project MATCH Research Group, "Matching Alcoholism Treatments to Client Heterogeneity: Project MATCH Three-Year Drinking Outcomes," *Alcoholism: Clinical & Experimental Research* 22, no. 6 (1998), 1300–11.

20. R. Longabaugh, P. W. Wirtz, A. Zweben, and R. L. Stout, "Network Support for Drinking, Alcoholics Anonymous and Long-term Matching Effects," *Addiction* 93, no. 9 (September 1998): 1313–33.

21. H. Clinton, *It Takes a Village* (New York: Simon & Schuster, 2006).

22. I. Johnson, "Alcohol Problems in Old Age: A Review of Recent Epidemiological Research," *International Journal of Geriatric Psychiatry* 15, no. 7 (July 2000): 575–81.

23. S. Ross, "Alcohol Use Disorders in the Elderly," *Primary Psychiatry* 12, no. 1 (2005).

24. "Wounded Warrior Project," 2011. http://www.woundedwarriorproject.org.

25. National Center for Complementary and Alternative Medicine, "Meditation: An Introduction," Publication No. D308 (2006). http://www.nccam.nih.gov.

26. B. Hölzel, J. Carmody, M. Vangel, C. Congleton, S. Yerramsetti, T. Gard, and S. Lazar, "Mindfulness Practice Leads to Increases in Regional Brain Gray Matter Density," *Psychiatry Research: Neuroimaging* 191, no. 1 (2011): 36–43.

27. J. Kabat-Zinn, *Wherever You Go, There You Are* (New York: Hyperion, 2005).

28. B. Carey, "Expert on Mental Illness Reveals Her Own Fight," *New York Times*, June 23, 2011. http://nyti.ms/kgaohw.

29. Johnson, "Alcohol Problems in Old Age."

30. "National Comorbidity Survey (NCS)," Harvard School of Medicine (2005). http://www.hcp.med.harvard.edu/ncs.

31. Ibid.

32. Project MATCH Research Group, "Matching Alcoholism Treatments to Client Heterogeneity."

33. Alcoholics Anonymous, *Alcoholics Anonymous*, 4th ed. (New York: Alcoholics Anonymous World Services, Inc., 2000), 31–32.

about the authors

Robert Doyle, MD, is a nationally recognized expert on alcoholism. He is a clinical instructor in psychiatry at Harvard Medical School and is on the medical staff at Harvard's prestigious teaching hospital, Massachusetts General Hospital. Dr. Doyle is also on the staff at Harvard University Health Services, where he counsels hundreds of Harvard students each year on alcohol-related problems, depression, anxiety, attention deficit hyperactivity disorder (ADHD), and other issues.

Joseph Nowinski, PhD, is a clinical psychologist. He has held positions as assistant professor of psychiatry at the University of California–San Francisco and associate adjunct professor of psychology at the University of Connecticut, and he is a columnist for *The Huffington Post* and *Psychology Today*. He is author of the *Twelve Step Facilitation Outpatient Program*, *Twelve Step Facilitation for the Dually Diagnosed Client*, and *The Family Recovery Program*, all published by Hazelden. Nowinski has a private practice in Tolland, Connecticut.

Hazelden, a national nonprofit organization founded in 1949, helps people reclaim their lives from the disease of addiction. Built on decades of knowledge and experience, Hazelden offers a comprehensive approach to addiction that addresses the full range of patient, family, and professional needs, including treatment and continuing care for youth and adults, research, higher learning, public education and advocacy, and publishing.

A life of recovery is lived "one day at a time." Hazelden publications, both educational and inspirational, support and strengthen lifelong recovery. In 1954, Hazelden published *Twenty-Four Hours a Day*, the first daily meditation book for recovering alcoholics, and Hazelden continues to publish works to inspire and guide individuals in treatment and recovery, and their loved ones. Professionals who work to prevent and treat addiction also turn to Hazelden for evidence-based curricula, informational materials, and videos for use in schools, treatment programs, and correctional programs.

Through published works, Hazelden extends the reach of hope, encouragement, help, and support to individuals, families, and communities affected by addiction and related issues.

For questions about Hazelden publications,
please call **800-328-9000** or visit us online
at **hazelden.org/bookstore.**